Your Answers to Education Questions

Ronald W. Holmes, Ph.D

Publisher, The Holmes Education Post, LLC
"An Education Focused Internet Newspaper"

AuthorHouse™ LLC
1663 Liberty Drive
Bloomington, IN 47403
www.authorhouse.com
Phone: 1-800-839-8640

Published by AuthorHouse 02/14/2014

ISBN: 978-1-4918-6507-1 (sc)
ISBN: 978-1-4918-6506-4 (e)

Library of Congress Control Number: 2014902936

CONTENTS

ACKNOWLEDGEMENT VII

DEDICATION IX

INTRODUCTION XI

REGARDING STUDENTS 1

    IS IT TIME TO TEACH KIDS ABOUT STRANGER SAFETY? 2

    IS IT TIME TO "STAND FOR THE SILENT?" 5

    IS IT TIME FOR RANDOM DRUG TESTING OF HIGH
        SCHOOL STUDENT-ATHLETES? 8

    WHAT SHOULD BE THE CIVIC MISSION OF U.S. PUBLIC SCHOOLS? ... 11

    WHY ARE SOME STUDENTS LESS LIKELY TO TAKE AP COURSES? 13

    HOW IS HAZING A PART OF THE K-12 CULTURE? 16

REGARDING TEACHERS 19

    WHAT IS AN ALTERNATIVE TO TEACHER CERTIFICATION? 20

    WHAT ARE THE NEW TEACHER EVALUATION PILOTS
        FOR OAKLAND UNIFIED SCHOOL DISTRICT? 23

    HOW CAN SCHOOLS UTILIZE EMPLOYEES' STRENGTHS
        TO IMPROVE PERFORMANCE IN THE WORKFORCE? 25

    IS IT TIME TO PLACE CAMERAS IN THE CLASSROOM? 28

REGARDING CURRICULUM 31

    IS IT TIME FOR MORE AFTERSCHOOL AND SUMMER
        LEARNING PROGRAMS? 32

    DOES ATHLETIC INVOLVEMENT IMPROVE ACADEMIC SUCCESS? 34

    WHAT MAKES DISD'S SCHOOL FOR THE TALENTED AND
        GIFTED THE TOP IN THE NATION? 36

    HOW CAN SCHOOLS IMPROVE EDUCATIONAL
        OPPORTUNITIES FOR MILITARY CHILDREN? 38

    WHY DID PUTNAM COUNTY SCHOOL DISTRICT
        IMPLEMENT THE SIXTH GRADE CENTER? 40

REGARDING SCHOOL SYSTEMS......44

   HOW CAN SCHOOLS PREPARE STUDENTS FOR A 21ST
     CENTURY WORKFORCE? 45

   HOW CAN SCHOOLS USE CONTENT MARKETING TO
     PROMOTE THEIR PROGRAMS AND SERVICES? 47

   HOW CAN SCHOOL DISTRICTS CREATE A CULTURE OF
     EXCELLENCE FOR ALL STUDENTS, STAFF AND FAMILIES? 50

   HOW DID DOUGLAS COUNTY SCHOOL DISTRICT AVOID
     A BUDGET CUT? 53

   IS IT TIME TO BAIL OUT U.S. SCHOOL DISTRICTS? 57

   WHAT IS REPLACING THE NO CHILD LEFT BEHIND LAW
     IN GEORGIA? 60

   WHAT SCHOOLS ARE HONOREES OF THE 2013 GREEN
     RIBBON SCHOOLS? 62

   HOW CAN SCHOOL DISTRICTS BENEFIT FROM A ZERO-
     BASED BUDGETING MODEL? 65

   IS IT TIME TO GRADE SCHOOL SYSTEMS' WEBSITES? 68

   WHO SHOULD HAVE THE POWER TO APPROVE
     CHARTER SCHOOLS? 70

REGARDING HIGHER EDUCATION 73

   HOW SHOULD GENERAL COUNSEL BE USED AT
     COLLEGES AND UNIVERSITIES? 74

   WHAT NEW MINDSETS ARE NEEDED TO HARNESS CHANGE? 77

   WHAT IS THE SUPREME COURT RULING OF THE FISHER
     V. TEXAS LEGAL CASE? 80

   HOW CAN THE NATION'S HIGHER EDUCATION BE
     RESTORED TO PREEMINENCE? 82

   HOW DO WE INCREASE THE DIVERSITY OF BUSINESS
     SCHOOL FACULTY? 85

ROADMAP FOR SUCCESSFUL & STRUGGLING SCHOOLS IN THE U.S. 88

REFERENCES 103
AUTHOR'S BACKGROUND 109

ACKNOWLEDGEMENT

I would like to thank all of the followers of The Holmes Education Post, an education focused Internet newspaper.

I would like to thank Reverend Dr. R.B. Holmes, Jr. and my wife, Constance Holmes for encouraging me to write a weekly education article in the Capital Outlook Newspaper. Reverend Holmes had the insight to create a radio and newspaper business and encouraged me to partner with him. He felt that the community needed an outlet for positive news as an avenue to uplift, empower and save the families. Constance was an invaluable resource in my life for helping me create The Holmes Education Post. She felt that the community needed to learn more about the numerous experiences I have gained as an educator, researcher and school leader.

I wholeheartedly thank Reverend Holmes and Constance for their inspiration, encouragement and support. I equally thank my parents, grandparents, siblings and other relatives who have been a springboard to my success. I have had a family that consistently supported me through the good and bad times.

Most importantly, I thank the Almighty God for sustaining me during my education and career path. He has been my source of strength, and I acknowledge his goodness and mercy in delivering me to this point.

DEDICATION

I proudly dedicate this book to my grandparents Clem and Louise Johnson. As a child in the 1960s, I gained real-world business experience from them while working in their grocery store in Americus, Georgia. They taught me to politely greet every customer who entered the store with the question, "Something for you?" In modern day vernacular, the question would be, "May I help you?"

In the same vein, I gratefully dedicate this book to my parents R.B. and Lucille Holmes. They have been the backbone to my achievement and accolades in all endeavors. They constantly taught me the value of prayer, life, family, school and work. Through the years, I learned so many lessons from them. Specifically, my father taught me about perseverance and credibility as he worked long hours and assisted his friends and three sons in getting good jobs with his employer. My mother taught me about fortitude as she set the example by going back to school and earning a college degree and teaching high school for over twenty-two years after raising eight children. Her perseverance showed me the value of education and taught me that it is never too late to pursue your dream. Her motivation influenced all of her children to attend college and earn a bachelor's degree.

Again, I dedicate this book to my grandparents and parents. I have achieved a life-time dream and an appreciation for life through their prayers, guidance, mentoring, coaching, teaching and giving to people. As such, all proceeds for this book will go towards scholarships for students.

INTRODUCTION

Through empirical research, this book provides educators and other followers of The Holmes Education Post, with solutions to education questions in our educational institutions. These solutions include 30 articles on some of our latest interventions to address challenges plaguing our institutions.

Each article provides the reader a question related to our educational institutions, references and reflections for the question. In a proposal format with an introduction, problem statement and solution to the problem, I have included a roadmap for successful and struggling schools in the United States with objectives, goals, strategies and performance measures. For better understanding, I have also linked some of the articles from this book to a strategy, as well as articles from my first two books on education: "Education Questions to be Answered" and "Current Issues and Answers in Education." It is hoped that the readers of this book will use the information to address the ongoing issues in education for improved student learning and instruction.

Regarding Students

Is it time to teach kids about stranger safety?

A "missing kid" is a frightening experience for any parent. According to the National Center for Missing and Exploited Children (NCMEC), 800,000 children younger than 18 are missing annually – an average of 2,185 children reported missing daily. Sixty-three percent of the abductions involve non-family members such as a babysitter, friend, long-term acquaintance, neighbor, caretaker or person of authority; whereas, 37 percent of the abductions involve a stranger. Most abductions occur during the day while a child is walking home or riding a bicycle between the hours of two and seven in the evening.

Considering the number of children reported missing, the critical questions to be asked are: Is it time to teach kids about stranger safety? What are safety tips for children and parents?

In a NBC special documentary, "My Kid Would Never Do That: Stranger Danger," elementary school kids were tested on what they would do when approached by a stranger. The kids were not aware they were being videotaped by NBC and watched by their parents. The children were only informed that they were participating in a community project to make posters for U.S. troops. The hope was that the kids would remember the things their parents taught them about getting into a vehicle with a stranger.

The kids participating in the experiment included the NBC reporter's own son, a set of twins, three girls who did not know each other and three boys that knew each other. The children were all faced with the same challenge: a stranger in an ice cream truck offers free ice cream and coerces them to come into the truck and look at the truck's music machine. All of the kids had been coached by their parents about the dangers of talking and accepting items from strangers. The results of the experiment were disappointing and scary.

Of the twins, one child was reluctant to get in the truck, refused to accept ice cream and expressed that they would have to ask their parents about the stranger's requests. The other twin took the ice cream. The three girls who did not know each other became very excited about the arrival of the ice cream truck. All of the girls followed the stranger to the back of the truck and one of them got into the truck, received her ice cream and started marveling over the truck's music machine. One of the three girls who had been taught repeatedly by her father (a police officer) about stranger safety, pulled the other girl away from the truck and told her that it was a scam. With the repeated coercing of the stranger, the two girls cautiously approached the side of the truck and reluctantly got ice cream from the stranger.

Of the three boys who were very good friends, one child stayed back (the NBC reporter's son) while the other two boys followed the stranger to the truck. Eventually, all three boys got their ice cream with the reporter's son running for safety behind the project area. All of the parents were disappointed with their children and realized they had to work more with them to help them understand the dangers of talking with strangers and accepting items from them.

To avoid potential abductions, NCMEC provides the following safety tips for children and parents: For children, they should (1) avoid being tricked by adults who offer special gifts or treats such as ice cream; (2) get approval from your parents before you go or do anything with a stranger; (3) say no to all requests by strangers and (4) take a friend when you go somewhere. Parents should (1) teach kids to avoid getting in or going towards a stranger's vehicle; (2) establish rules for where they can go in the neighborhood (3) practice role-playing various scenarios and (4) keep open lines of communication.

Similarly, the NBC expert on abductions noted that parents should teach kids at a young age how to say no and be assertive and strong when approached by strangers. She also noted that parents should place emphasis on teaching kids about different abduction situations such as what to say if a stranger says, "Don't tell your parents."

Keeping our children safe is a major responsibility of parents. In today's environment, our children can be faced with untold scams that can ultimately harm them mentally and physically. As parents, we must diligently train our children about how to handle strangers and the actions they can take when they are in dangerous situations.

Is it time to "Stand for the Silent?"

The famous expression, "sticks and stones may break my bones but words shall never harm me" is obsolete in this day and time for many public school students. One third of today's middle and high school students report being bullied through verbal and physical means. In fact, it is estimated that 13 million children are bullied each year. Bullying is a serious epidemic causing students to drop out of school, commit a crime or take their own lives. For this column, the question to be asked is: Is it time to "Stand for the Silent?"

Similar to hazing, bullying is a dangerous act that degrades, humiliates and harms a person mentally or physically. Although hazing differs from bullying in that it pertains to an individuals' participation in a group, bullying is a part of the hazing rituals and comes in different forms. Sexting and cyber bullying are the new age type of bullying. In a national iSAFE study of fourth to eight graders, 42 percent of these students suffered the impact of cyber bullying through electronic devices such as cell phones and the internet. In many instances, these inappropriate acts are coordinated before students enter the school buildings.

As a result, school leaders must be more transparent in their day-to-day routines and reinforce school policies with faculty members and students in multiple ways such as assemblies, pep rallies, meetings and class periods throughout the academic year. School leaders must communicate these same policies to parents and community constituents such as law enforcement and social service agencies for improved accountability. Ultimately, school leaders must build strong relationships with their students so that they become compelled to inform the authorities of any form of bigotry or harassment confronting their safety, health or life.

In the documentary movie "Bully," by Lee Hirsch, the public sees a compelling view of the effects of bullying. This movie depicts the tragedies of students who have been affected mentally and physically by their bullies, as well as the seriousness of the problem across ethnic, geographical and economic boundaries.

First, there is Alex, a timid 12-year old seventh grader from Sioux City, Iowa who was repeatedly threatened on the school bus, called offensive names such as "Fish Face" and punched by his perpetrators. To avoid making waves, Alex tells his concerned parents the classmates are "just messing with him." Second, there is Kelby, a 16-year old high school basketball star-athlete from Tuttle, Oklahoma. Kelby was ridiculed when she announced being a lesbian, called derogatory names such as "faggot" and faced bigotry by stakeholders at the school. Kelby was determined to remain in Tuttle despite her parents' wishes to leave the city to avoid the unnecessary and unwanted abuse by her bullies.

Third, there is Ja'Meya, a quiet 14-year old girl from Yazoo County, Mississippi who was repeatedly teased by her bullies on the school bus. Pushed to the brink, Ja'Meya took her mother's handgun on the school bus to stop her perpetrators. She was charged with multiple felony counts and placed in a juvenile detention facility. Fourth, there is the story of 17-year old Tyler from Murray County, Georgia who was overpowered by the bullying acts of classmates, indifferences of school officials and hanged himself in his parent's home. According to Tyler's father, David Long, "I knew he would be victimized at some point in time. He had a target on his back. Everybody knew that."

Finally, there is the story of Ty, an 11-year old from Perkins, Oklahoma who committed suicide as result of bullying. His grief stricken parents, Kirk and Laura Smalley, are determined to prevent other children from been tormented from bullying and launched an anti-bullying organization called "Stand for the Silent." According to the father: "We are nobody and if it had been some politician's son, there would be a law tomorrow."

If you have ever lost a loved one, particularly, a child to a tragedy, it is a feeling that can take your breath away, so to speak. Some people never get over it and others seek some level of peace by organizing civic activities to address the issue.

The movie, "Bully" brings needed attention to this issue and calls for a nation to act.

In my view, it will take a multi-disciplined approach to address the bullying in our society. It must begin with educating all parties such as students, parents, teachers, administrators and community on how to handle the issue. Schools must have strong anti-bullying policies bolstered by laws that have strong sentences for this inappropriate behavior. Finally, it will take a community at large to raise the conscious of everyone that bullying will not be tolerated against our children. In this era, bullying is not just a part of "growing up or children being children." It is the number one problem confronting schools and must be eradicated.

Parents such as the Smalley's are calling on people across the nation to "Stand for the Silent" to end bullying and save children's lives. This campaign encourages children to become aware of the danger of bullying and inform authorities when they see bullying occurring. With the alarming rate of kids being victimized by bullying, it is time that we all "Stand for the Silent" and eliminate bullying from our culture.

Is it time for random drug testing of high school student-athletes?

Some advocates believe that the use of drugs improves sports by giving athletes a competitive edge while others believe drugs damage the game as well as the health and safety of athletes. To combat these drug issues, professional sports such as football and basketball have initiated random drug testing. Knowing that random drug testing is commonplace in professional sports, the critical questions to be asked are: Is it time for random drug testing of high school student-athletes? What legal cases support the use of random student drug testing? What does research say about the value of random student drug testing? What are the cost implications of testing?

Random drug testing of students can come in different forms such as urine or hair samplings to test for marijuana, cocaine, PCP, opiates, methamphetamine, etc. During random testing, participating schools select a random sample of students from the school population who participate in competitive extracurricular activities. The goal of drug abuse programs for participating schools is to successfully reduce drug abuse among students. This is done by deterring students from using drugs, identifying students who are using drugs and providing appropriate interventions and treatment services to combat drug abuse according to the National Institute on Drug Abuse.

While student privacy is a major issue, two U.S. Supreme Court cases in 1995 and 2002 supported school districts' position for random drug testing of high school students participating in competitive extracurricular activities. From these cases, the Supreme Court cited that deterring student drug use was more important than student privacy.

Based on a 2008 report by the Student Drug Testing Coalition, approximately 16.5 percent of U.S. school districts participate in random student drug testing programs. School districts in New Jersey and Kansas City are proposing random drug testing for their high school students. Specifically, Rockhurst High School in Kansas City is participating in mandatory random drug testing using hair samples for the 2013-2014 school year according to a report by Fox News. Principal Greg Harkness was cited saying, "Our point is, if we do encounter a student who has made some bad decisions with drugs or alcohol, we will be able to intervene, get the parents involved, get him help if necessary, and then help him get back on a path of better decision making and healthier choices for his life."

Research studies have looked at the effects of school districts' students participating in drug testing programs compared to students who did not participate in these programs. For example, the findings of a 2010 study released by the National Center for Education Evaluation comprising of seven school districts with 36 high schools and more than 4700 students found: (1) "students involved in extracurricular activities and subject to mandatory-random student drug testing reported less substance use than comparable students in high schools without drug testing and (2) the program had no "spillover effects" on the substance use reported by students who were not subject to testing and had no effect on any group of students' reported intentions to use substances in the future." In a 2003 ground-breaking study at the University of Michigan, slightly more students at schools with drug-testing policies (21 percent) were using drugs than students at schools without drug testing policies (19 percent) according to a report by Global Post.

In a stiff economy, school districts have to make sure that their funds are spent wisely and, at the same time, maintain the academic performance, health and safety of their students. Drug testing administered at the high school level cost between $15 to $35 dollars per student. According to a report by The New York Times, The Florida High School Athletic Association began drug testing 600 student athletes at a cost of $100,000 in 2007 but ended the testing program due to inadequate funding within the first year. The Illinois High School Association started drug testing 650 students at a cost of $100,000 in the 2008-2009 school year and found no positive test results. Also, the University Interscholastic League in Texas drug tested 10,117 student athletes in the 2007-2008 school year but reduced its testing sample to 3,311 student-athletes four years later due to budgetary pressures. Of this sample, nine student-athletes tested positive for drug use.

When we learn of students testing positive for using performance-enhancing drugs and subsequently becoming ill or losing their lives, this adds to the concern or debate for more random drug testing of high school students-athletes. In the famous expression of former first lady Nancy Reagan, schools should encourage all of their students to, "Just say no" to drugs. Schools must also employ various treatment interventions and counseling services, as well as establish partnerships with drug-free professional athletes through the National Football League, National Basketball Association, etc. to serve as role models for high school student-athletes.

What should be the civic mission of U.S. public schools?

Laws created under the Harm Principle are written to protect people from being harmed by others. Laws against violent crime and property crime fall into this category. Just as laws are created, they can also be abused.

Florida's "Stand Your Ground" law is an example of a Harm Principle law. When laws are flawed or unclear, it is imperative that they be repealed. To ensure that laws are written in the best interest of all people, American students must be taught at an early age the value of government policies and civic responsibility. In fact, they must learn and participate in civic activities to help define U.S. policies in the best interest of all humankind.

Just as schools are responsible for preparing students for college and careers, they are equally responsible for preparing students for civic learning and democratic engagement. This is supported by the National Task Force on Civic Learning and Democratic Engagement, the American Commonwealth Partnership and the Campaign for the Civic Mission of Schools in its 2011 report, Guardian of Democracy: The Civic Mission of Schools. This report notes that civic learning promotes civic knowledge, skills, and dispositions and builds the 21st century competencies that employers value of workers and is associated with a better school environment and lower student dropout rates according to the U.S. Department of Education (USDOE).

In contrast, a study of the National Assessment of Education Progress reported low academic performance in civics by elementary and secondary students, a significant achievement gap between racial and ethnic groups and a decline in civic knowledge of seniors in high schools between 2006 and 2010. The McCormick Tribune Foundation also reported in 2007 that the U.S. ranked 139th in voter participation compared to 172 democracies suggesting that Americans are inadequately involved in civic actions according to USDOE.

With public school students lacking civic readiness and inactivity in community involvement, the USDOE proposes a number of steps to help expand and elevate civic learning and engagement in democracy. Two of these steps include (1) supporting civic learning for a well-rounded K-12 curriculum and (2) highlighting and promoting student and family participation in education programs and policies at the federal and local levels. In the first step, USDOE emphasizes the importance of a well-rounded education with civic and service-learning components through a competitive program called Effective Teaching and Learning for a Well-Rounded Education. The program is to be part of the reauthorization of the Elementary and Secondary Education Act. In the second step, USDOE proposes to make government more transparent, collaborative and participatory in policymaking and implementing programs such as the School Improvement Grants and Promise Neighborhood to help address and provide solutions to issues confronting American communities.

Today's students appear to have fallen further away from political and social involvement. It is quite evident that students know and use social media but they do not know social responsibility. In fact, too often our communities are oblivious to government policies and community issues until there is a calamity. American students need service-learning activities to better understand the world. They need exposure to civic responsibility at an early age to become an integral part of the political process to prevent laws such as "Stand Your Ground" from being written and, subsequently, misinterpreted whether intentional or unintentional. Our future leaders of America must learn and participate in civic activities to help define U.S. policies in the best interest of all humankind.

Why are some students less likely to take AP courses?

The unemployment rate is 8.9 percent for college graduates with bachelor degrees, 22.9 percent for high school graduates and 31.5 percent for high school dropouts according to a study by the Georgetown Center on Education and Workforce. However, jobs in the areas of science, technology, engineering and mathematics (STEM) are projected to rise to 8 million by 2018. With this disparity, the critical questions to be asked are: Why are some students less likely to take Advanced Placement (AP) courses? What is the AP STEM Access program and how can it help prepare students for college and career success? How are public schools eligible for participation in the AP STEM Access program?

The College Board's Advanced Placement Program© provides eager and academically prepared students the opportunity to pursue college-level studies, develop critical thinking skills and earn advanced placement and/or college credit while in high school. Research indicates that when students score 3 or higher on an AP Exam, they perform better in college, are more likely to earn a college degree and are likely to be better prepared to take on the highly paid STEM jobs.

However, traditionally underrepresented students such as African Americans, Hispanic/Latinos, American Indian/Alaska Natives and females are less likely to take AP courses and, therefore, receive inadequate engagement in rigorous course work during high school. According to the College Board, in 2011 only 3 in 10 African American, Hispanic/Latino students and 2 in 10 American Indian/ Alaska Native students participated in AP mathematics courses. In that same year, there were more male students than female students taking AP Exams in calculus, chemistry, computer science and physics. When this happens, these students are less likely to study math and science in college and pursue STEM jobs.

So, why does this disparity exist? In many cases, College Board reports that students did not take AP math and science courses because they were not available at their schools and in scenarios where the courses exist, minority and female students simply did not participate. The diversity of AP classrooms frequently did not reflect the diversity of the school overall.

As a result, College Board announced the AP STEM Access program, created to increase the number of traditionally underrepresented minority and female high school students who participate in AP Program's courses in STEM disciplines (biology, calculus, chemistry, computer science, etc.). As part of its Global Impact Awards, Google is providing a $5 million grant to DonorsChoose.org, making it possible for this program to invite 819 public high schools across 22 states to start new AP math and science courses for a minimum of three years and to encourage traditionally underrepresented minority and female students who demonstrate strong academic potential to enroll and explore these areas of study and related careers.

To be selected for the program, these 800 schools were chosen because they have historically had a population of underrepresented students who were academically prepared for an AP STEM course that was not offered by the school. Specifically, in the 2010-11 academic year these schools had 10 or more African American, Hispanic/Latino, or American Indian/Alaska Native students — and/or 25 or more female students — with high potential to be successful in one or more AP STEM courses that were not offered in their school. In addition, these schools serve communities with a median household income of $100,000 or less, and/or 40 percent or more of their students qualify for free or reduced-price school meals. For this criterion, high AP potential was defined as a 70 percent or higher likelihood of scoring a 3, 4 or 5 on the AP Exam as predicted by the student's performance on specific sections of the PSAT/NMQST® (Preliminary SAT/National Merit Scholarship Qualifying Test), according to Potoula Chresomales, executive director of the Advanced Placement Program at the College Board. The state of Florida has a total of 109 qualifying schools, placing it among the top four states with the largest number of eligible schools in the country for the AP STEM Access program. For a listing of the schools, go to: www.collegeboard.org/APSTEM.

Prior to the start of the new AP courses in the Fall 2013, teachers at these schools will receive scholarships for professional development at an AP Summer Institute located at over 100 colleges and universities across the nation. Teachers will also be able to fund educational resources such as classroom materials, textbooks and technology equipment for the AP courses through DonorsChoose.org.

Representatives of Google and DonorsChoose.org expressed their excitement about the program. Jacquelline Fuller, director of giving at Google said, "There are hundreds of thousands of talented students in this country who are being left out of the STEM equation — they're not being given the opportunity to find their passion or pursue today's most promising careers. We're focused on creating equal access to advanced math and science courses, and ensuring that advanced classrooms become as diverse as the schools themselves."

The economy is in demand of a competent and competitive workforce and American schools must rise to the standards. If your public high school has traditionally underrepresented minority and female students who have been identified to have success in completing AP courses, you are encouraged to take advantage of this opportunity funded by Google and supported by College Board and DonorsChoose.org.

How is hazing a part of the K-12 culture?

The Super Bowl is one of the most exciting entertainment events of the year. It represents the best two football teams competing for the coveted Super Bowl Championship title. Advertisers see it as the time to promote their products because of the number of television viewers that will see their wares. Those fortunate few who get an opportunity to attend the games will spend an estimated $5,000 - $16,000 for a weekend trip. Even those who watch from home will spend an average of $60. By the time the three-hour game is over, the economy will experience a spend of $10 billion. The super bowl is a major part of the American culture and represents entertainment at its highest level.

So the critical questions to be asked are: How is hazing a part of the K-12 educational culture? What are school districts doing to ensure policies against hazing are followed? What actions have school districts taken to deter or address hazing incidents? Just as spending gregariously is a part of the Super Bowl culture, participating in extra-curricular activities and being hazed by perpetrators have been documented in studies at the University of Maine and Alfred University as being part of the K-12 culture particularly for middle and high school students. In these studies, students reported participating in hazing because it enabled them to feel closer as a group, provided approval by their peers and afforded an opportunity for revenge. Other students took part in hazing rituals because they were ill-informed, uneducated about what constitutes hazing behavior, pressured and influenced by the culture of the environment.

DeKalb County School System (DCSS) in Georgia and Nassau County School District (NCSD) in Florida are two school systems that are taking proactive measures to ensure that their policies against hazing are followed. On Dec. 14, 2011, DeKalb County suspended their entire student marching band activities at 19 schools to investigate allegations of "inappropriate behavior" in the marching band programs. The investigation started after several of Florida A&M University's students, who were graduates of Dekalb County, were either victimized of hazing activities at the university or charged for participating in hazing activities. After a preliminary investigation, DeKalb lifted the suspension on January 18, 2012.

During the investigation, Superintendent Dr. Cheryl Atkinson stated, however, that DCSS will continue to "ensure policies against intimidation and harassment are being followed; and at this stage, senior staff is confident that student activities can go on as planned. We have met with our high school principals and band directors to ensure everyone understands their responsibilities in terms of protecting our students, and that we all are accountable for enforcing school system policies when it comes to students and band activity."

At the end of 2011, Fernandina Beach High School had incidents of hazing when upper class wrestling team members paddled a newer member giving the victim "red-bellies." In reaction to the occurrence of hazing, Superintendent John Ruis said that the district was "looking to strengthen its policies on hazing with a higher classification of offense from a class III to a class IV offense." The district also will "revise or amend its bullying and harassment policies to incorporate or add hazing in its administrative rules."

While no employees at DeKalb County were reprimanded for any wrongdoing associated with the marching band programs, two wrestling coaches at Nassau County were terminated from their coaching duties after being suspended from those roles during the investigation, according to Ruis.

Hazing is illegal in 44 states and comprises of "any activity expected of someone to join a group that has the potential to humiliate, degrade, abuse or endanger a person regardless of his or her willingness to participate" in the activity. While extra-curricular activities contribute to students' performance in school, unacceptable initiation activities are on the rise at the secondary level. Students have multiple ways to collectively initiate or plan hazing activities towards individuals using high tech methods such as cyber bullying and sexting. In many instances, these inappropriate acts are coordinated before students enter the school buildings. In a national iSAFE study of fourth to eighth graders, 42 percent of these students were harassed through cyber bullying.

As a result, school leaders must be more transparent in their day-to-day routines and reinforce school policies with faculty members and students in multiple ways such as assemblies, pep rallies, meetings, class periods, etc. throughout the academic year. School leaders must also communicate these same policies to parents and community constituents such as alumni members for improved accountability. Ultimately, school leaders must build strong relationships with their students so that they become compelled to inform the authorities of any form of harassment or intimidation confronting their safety, health or life.

Just as the Super Bowl is a cultural event, hazing has cultural components. In order to eradicate this behavior, it will take a multidiscipline approach to address the problem. It must begin with educating all parties such as students, parents, teachers and administrators. In addition, schools must have strong policies bolstered by laws that have strong sentences for these acts of violence. Finally, it will take a community at large to raise the conscious of everyone that hazing and violence will not be tolerated against our children.

Regarding Teachers

What is an alternative to teacher certification?

Hundreds of thousands of aging baby boomers are expected to retire in the next ten years leaving school districts with lots of openings to fill. According to the National Center for Education Statistics, nearly 500,000 new hires will be required to fill both public and private school teaching jobs by the year 2018. As one avenue to fill this void, the Florida Department of Education has created the Educator Preparation Institute that prepares mid-career professionals and college graduates who are not education majors to obtain teacher certification. For this article, I interviewed Dr. Betty Bennett, director of University of North Florida's (UNF) Educator Preparation Institute to answer the critical questions: What is the University of North Florida's Educator Preparation Institute, an alternative to teacher certification? Why was the Institute established at UNF? What has been the success of the Educator Preparation Institute?

UNF's Educator Preparation Institute:

The Education Preparation Institute (EPI) is a ten-month program combining instructional modules, field experiences and mentoring. The program allows individuals who have had former careers, or have obtained a degree and decided they don't want to follow that profession or can't find employment, and would like to become educators, to do so. Instead of going back for another bachelor's degree, they can come through the EPI, take the three subtests of the Florida Teachers Competency Exam, complete a field experience and gain a Florida Professional Teacher Certificate. The UNF's EPI runs from August – June and meets every other Saturday, except holiday weekends, for a total of 20 sessions, from 9:00 a.m. -3:15 p.m. Students also complete a field experience in a public school with a principal recommended Mentor Teacher. Each student is required to spend a minimum of 60 hours in the mentor teacher's classroom. Upon completion of the program, students are eligible to apply to the state for their professional certificate.

Establishment of the Educator Preparation Institute:

Initially the state allowed universities and community colleges (now state colleges) to submit proposals to begin alternative certification programs. This was in response to the state's efforts to address critical teacher shortages. Despite the economic difficulties, critical shortages remain in areas such as mathematics, science, special education, reading, foreign language and others depending on geographic area. In addition, there is a need for highly qualified individuals. The EPI holds special advantages in that many of our students, as career changers, bring with them experience and degrees with specific content. Some of our students come to us with degrees in chemistry, accounting, English, biology, law, medicine, aerospace, mathematics, engineering, technology, physics, foreign languages and more. One of our current students came to us with a Bachelor of Business Administration, Master of Business Administration, Juris Doctorate and Medical Doctor. He is a retiring physician who has always wanted to be a teacher. He has a passion for service and would like to give back to the community. We also have many retired military veterans who enter the program. We are Veterans Administration approved so they can use their benefits to complete the program. Veterans are successful in the classroom due to their focus on structure and organization.

Success of the Educator Preparation Institute:

In the last report released by the Florida Department of Education in June, our UNF graduates out-performed other EPIs in hiring, retention rates and scored 17 percent higher in math than the statewide mean for EPI program graduates.

Our biggest success is being affiliated with UNF. We also pride ourselves with having a quality program that is concerned with listening to our constituents and growing with this feedback every year. Our curriculum coordinator comes with 40 plus years of experience that she pours into the program with very little pay. We have grown each year because of the quality of the people completing the program and gaining positions in our school districts. The confidence is growing with our surrounding community as the quality of our graduates continues to spread. The fact that the students who enter our program are of optimum quality adds to the mix. Students admitted to the program, write an essay reflecting why they wish to become a teacher. I read each one. If it doesn't reflect a definite passion for education and the students they will teach, they are not admitted regardless of their other credentials. If there is a glimmer, I call them in for an interview. Unless there is some other glaring difficulty, passion is the ultimate criterion.

What are the new Teacher Evaluation pilots for Oakland Unified School District?

To meet accountability standards, school districts are exploring best practices to evaluate their teachers and, subsequently, increase student achievement. While identifying an appropriate evaluation model with the involvement of the teacher association is essential, the critical questions to be asked are: What are the new Teacher Evaluation pilots for Oakland Unified School District (OUSD)? How will OUSD study the Teacher Evaluation Pilots?

Collectively, A Nation at Risk Report of 1983, the Educate America Act of 1994, the No Child Left Behind Act of 2001 and the Race to the Top grant program, all have played a role in shaping the expectations for evaluation systems and school accountability. According to research, school districts with successful evaluation systems ensure that all parties of the district understand the instrument and consistently use the results from the instrument. In addition, these school districts require that the evaluation systems are interwoven with the district's mission, focus on student achievement and ensure that professional development and teacher evaluation are connected and continuous.

The Oakland Unified School District and the Oakland Education Association (OEA) will begin piloting a new Teacher Evaluation for the 2013-2014 school year. OUSD and OEA are seeking an evaluation model that will make the teacher evaluation process more personalized, transparent and easily understood. They are also seeking a model that reflects improvement in teacher instruction and student achievement. Before arriving at a final evaluation model, both the school district and teacher association also acknowledged that it will take time to create a model that is informative, reliable and implemented correctly. As such, both parties have established a Memorandum of Understanding (MOU) regarding the pilot.

One of the stipulations in the MOU is to formulate a Joint Study Committee. The committee's function is to document and discuss the findings from the Teacher Evaluation pilots. It will also analyze the current evaluation model as it is implemented in non-participating schools. By May 2014, the committee is expected to provide a preliminary report regarding what worked, what did not work and what should be studied further in Oakland Unified School District.

Similarly, the State of New Jersey Department of Education announced in 2011 its pilot evaluation system to grade teachers in 31 school districts. The goal was to establish a framework that can evaluate teachers based on multiple measures of teacher practice and student performance and be used to implement a new evaluation system for all school districts in New Jersey for the upcoming school year (s). According to Commissioner Chris Cerf, the findings of the pilot reflect that educators are having more meaningful conversations than previously to foster effective teaching and learning in these schools.

How can schools utilize employees' strengths to improve performance in the workforce?

If "one bad apple does not spoil a show," what should you do with the apple? Some people would say that you should get rid of the apple. Others would say, endure the apple or place the apple with other bad apples. When you consider real-world scenarios, school leaders may either fire an ineffective employee, tolerate the employee or transfer the employee to another setting to allow someone else to deal with the problem.

So, the questions to be asked are: How can schools use employees' strengths to improve performance in the workplace? Is it possible to take what is unique about the employee and make them useful? How can author Marcus Buckingham's nine strength roles be used to maximize employees' contributions to the workplace?

At a workshop by author Marcus Buckingham, he discusses the concepts of focusing on strengths. According to Buckingham, we each have specific areas where we consistently "standout," where we can do things, see things, understand things and learn things better and faster than other people can. Buckingham says that when we find ourselves in these "strength zones," we are magnificent, self-assured and flushed with success. The objective then is for the employee and the manager to understand the unique strengths and to focus and harness those strengths in the workplace. Simply put, Buckingham says "you are most productive and creative in those areas where you are already strong." So, organizations of all types, including schools, should focus on employees' strengths rather than their weaknesses to make them feel useful in the organizations in order to improve performance.

As a vehicle to assess the uniqueness of employees, Buckingham created the "Standout" assessment that measures you on nine strength roles. Through a questionnaire, the assessment highlights your top two roles. They are seen as your greatest contributions and the "edge" you have on other employees in the organization. These roles include advisor, connector, creator, equalizer, influencer, pioneer, provider, stimulator and teacher. Buckingham notes that in the teacher role, "you are thrilled by the potential you see in each person. Your power comes from learning how to unleash it." In contrast, Buckingham says that in the stimulator role, "you are the host of other people's emotions. You feel responsible for them, for turning them around and for elevating them."

Specifically, Buckingham explains that in the questionnaire, you are asked to respond to different scenarios. He says that these scenarios were captured from stakeholders in industries of all types over the past 10 years. The results of your choices are how teammates view you rather than how you view yourself.

According to research, only 20 percent of employees utilize their true talents in their organizations. Buckingham suggests that businesses should harness their employees' strengths and make their employees' weaknesses obsolete. They should have discourse continuously to determine best practices for getting the job done proficiently in the organizations.

Buckingham notes that this might include benchmarking best practices from various organizations then using those practices that best fit their organizations. He gives examples of how a best practice may work effectively in one organization but may not work the same in another organization. So the key is to make sure that the practice you adopt is germane to your organization.

To illustrate, Buckingham articulates how several hotel industries use various approaches, such as mascots and symbols, to improve performance in their organizations through the contributions of their employees. He emphasizes, however, that hotel "A" could not use hotel "X" business profile identically because the climate of the two organizations are not the same. In order to transfer one business profile to another organization, Buckingham says that you have to grasp the understanding of the best practice and then make it fit your organizational profile. You cannot mix apples and oranges and expect the same result of another organization.

From a school perspective, Buckingham's concepts can be applicable. For example, school districts are faced with budgetary shortfalls. Research reports that policymakers in numerous states are providing flexibility to school districts to change their instructional calendar. Thus, the four-day school week provides a key best practice for when there are limited options in the school district budget. However, each school district has to assess the pros and cons of the best practice and then determine if the practice is relevant to its organizational profile.

As it is written, "one bad apple does not spoil a show." There are alternatives for dealing with the apple. Using Marcus Buckingham's theory, every apple has its own uniqueness. When we recognize the apple's strengths and focus on those strengths, there is where the genius lies. Marcus Buckingham's view of strengths is applicable to the school environment, whether we are focusing on employees or applying the concept to children. The ultimate goal is get the best performance out of people. The essential point is that people are most efficient and innovative when they operate in their strength zones rather than their weakness zones. By focusing on the concept of strengths, people can activate their unique competitive advantage in the workplace.

Is it time to place cameras in the classroom?

Twenty-two percent of all traffic accidents in the U.S. are caused by drivers who run red lights and 39 percent of these accidents result in injuries according to the Insurance Institute for Highway Safety. Because of a shortage of human resources to monitor motorists coupled with the rise in traffic violations, accidents, fatalities, property damages and insurance hikes, cities nationwide are installing red-light cameras. Cameras allow authorities to prosecute traffic violators by detecting speeding as well as minimizing disputes regarding the violation. Motorists receive a ticket in the mail along with a photograph of the violation.

Just as cameras are being used to monitor motorists, school systems are considering the use of cameras in the classroom to monitor teachers. So the questions to be asked are: Is it time to place cameras in the classroom to evaluate teachers' performance? What are the pros and cons of placing cameras in the classroom? Why are some parents requesting that cameras be placed in the classroom?

In 2011, the Legislature in Wyoming proposed to have cameras installed in the classrooms to measure the performance of teachers' evaluations, however, it was rejected at the Senate level. In 2009, the Bill and Melinda Gates Foundation launched the Measures of Effective Teaching project to pilot test new strategies for measuring effective teaching through videotaping of 20,000 classroom lessons of 3,000 volunteer teachers in six urban school districts across the country. The videotaping of classroom lessons through agencies such as the National Board for Professional Teaching Standards has in the past and present been used as an instructional tool for teachers' professional development and national board certification. The idea to have cameras in the classroom to evaluate the performance of teachers is appalling to some and appealing to others.

Some critics believe that cameras in the classroom will create an atmosphere that will catch a teacher doing something wrong whether intentional or unintentional. In addition, they believe that having cameras will add stress and take away the personal interaction of the principal, teacher and student in the evaluation process. Finally, there are concerns that cameras will violate student and teacher privacy.

Proponents of cameras in the classroom believe that cameras will help assess the effectiveness of the classroom by creating a record for principals and teachers, and thus, minimizing any dispute regarding the evaluation process. Proponents also feel that the recordings can show clear evidence for professional development in the areas of need. Other proponents claim cameras will improve instructional processes and accountability and eliminate the potential of inappropriate behavior of students and teachers in the educational environment.

As an example of camera use, in 2003 the Biloxi Public School District in Biloxi, Mississippi installed cameras in all of its schools' hallways and classrooms primarily for the improvement of safety. These schools now report lower incidents of violence and less dozing off in class, which may translate into higher student performance. Parents in Los Angeles School District (2012) vehemently requested cameras in the classrooms and other areas of the school when they learned of two teachers who were arrested for allegedly allowing lewd acts by students. The entire staff of a Los Angeles elementary school was reassigned to fully address the problem and avoid any additional surprises.

Additionally, a parent in New Jersey (2012) received reports from the school claiming his autistic child was making violent outbursts and displaying disruptive behavior in the classroom. Realizing the 10 year-old child was mild-mannered and non-violent, the parent wired his son, sent him to school and listened to the audio tape once his son returned home. Consequently, the parent reported to the school district his hearing on the tape of a teacher and aide bullying his son through humiliation, name-calling and repeated yelling which led to the employees being removed from the school. This is an example of a parent finding value in having a recording of the classroom setting.

While we are in a society where the use of cameras is becoming commonplace, the issue of cameras in the classroom is a very sensitive and complex matter confronting school districts especially when you consider the need for students and teachers' privacy and the accountability of schools to maintain academic excellence and zero tolerance for inappropriate behavior in the classroom. We must tread cautiously to consider whether the pros outweigh the cons for using cameras in the classroom -- whether it is for teacher evaluation, professional development or safety of students and teachers. The answer to the question is not clear cut and must be determined by the issue to be solved.

Regarding Curriculum

Is it time for more afterschool and summer learning programs?

Home Alone is the 1990 family comedy film of an eight-year old boy (Kevin McCallister played by Macaulay Culkin) who was mistakenly left behind in the home as his parents rushed to the airport to make their flight to Paris for a Christmas vacation. While unsupervised, Kevin engaged in inappropriate behavior such as watching a gangster movie, eating excessive junk food and shooting his brother's BB gun. To add to the comedy, Kevin outwits and defends himself from two burglars trying to rob his home.

Being left at home is nothing new for many children who are the products of working parents. It is estimated that 15.1 million children in the U.S. are left home alone and unsupervised. So the critical questions to be asked are: Is it time for more afterschool and summer learning programs? What services do afterschool and summer learning programs provide to African-American and Latino communities? What is the 21st Century Community Learning Centers Federal Afterschool Initiative?

Communities nationwide are cutting programs at parks and recreational facilities. Our youth and particularly, disadvantaged children, are faced with unmet needs in their homes and communities. Recent data from the Afterschool Alliance, a nonprofit public awareness advocacy organization working to ensure that all children and youth have access to quality afterschool programs, notes that "afterschool and summer learning programs are valuable vehicles to help address elevated rates of poverty, homelessness, unemployment and food insecurity in African-American and Latino communities." These programs serve as a means to complement educational activities offered during the school day rather than reproduce them.

It is estimated that 8.4 million children participate in afterschool programs. Specifically, afterschool and summer learning programs provide services to the African-American and Latino communities by: (1) ensuring children have access to academically enriching activities, helping close the opportunity gap between higher-income and lower-income families; (2) tackling the achievement gap among White, African-American and Latino students by increasing attendance, homework completion and engagement in school, and ultimately raising graduation rates and test scores; (3) combating food insecurity among children by providing nutritious snacks and meals, which are especially important during the summer months when schools are out of session and (4) providing working parents with the peace of mind that comes from knowing that their children are in a safe and supervised space during the out-of-school hours, according to the Afterschool Alliance.

Afterschool Alliance Executive Director Jodi Grant said, "Afterschool and summer learning programs play a vital role in supporting youth and families in underserved and struggling communities. But the unmet demand for afterschool and summer programs in minority communities is a huge barrier to progress. We need to expand funding so that all children can have access to the high-quality afterschool and summer learning programs that keep kids safe, inspire students to learn and help working families."

While there are a variety of afterschool programs such as YMCA, Boys and Girls Clubs, the 21st Century Community Learning Centers ((21st CCLC) is the only federal funding source earmarked exclusively to afterschool programs. As a component of the No Child Left Behind Act in 2002, state education agencies receive funding from the U.S. Department of Education based on its share of Title I appropriation for low-income students. These grants also support afterschool programs by offering academic enrichment activities and services to reinforce and complement the regular academic program. Since its inception, more than 4,000 grants have been funded for approximately 1.6 million children and youth in 10,000 school and community-based centers throughout the country. The funding for 21st CCLC is 1.54 billion. If your state education agency is not participating in the afterschool program or you desire to learn additional information about this initiative, please go to the Afterschool Alliance website: http://www.afterschoolalliance.org/policyNCLB.cfm.

Does athletic involvement improve academic success?

Learning comes in different forms. Schools typically foster learning by employing highly qualified teachers and principals, using data to drive instruction, integrating technology in the curriculum and involving students in extra-curricular activities. While schools are challenged by societal demands to improve education and subsequently prepare students for college, careers and life, the critical question to be asked is: Does athletic involvement improve academic success?

In a 2011-2012 national study, Dr. Anthony Price, Jr. along with the National Interscholastic Athletic Administrators Association (NIAAA) analyzed the academic success of nearly 700,000 high school student-athletes and non-student athletes in 961 schools. Academic success was determined by four indicators: graduation rates, dropout rates, average daily attendance and average letter grades. Athletic involvement was defined as a student-athlete participating in a school sponsored sports' team; whereas a student who did not participate in a sponsored sports' team was considered a non-student athlete.

The study's findings indicated a significant correlation between athletic involvement and academic success as indicated by graduation rates, dropout rates, average daily attendance and average letter grades. Graduation rates ranked the highest according to significance during the study followed by dropout rates, average daily attendance and average letter grades. Respectively, non-student athletes earned a 2.72 grade point average (GPA) while student-athletes earned an overall 3.01 GPA. In every category of this national study's four indicators, it demonstrated that schools with higher student-athletes involvement achieved better than schools with higher non student-athletes.

As a former coach, teacher and school leader, I saw first-hand how students who were involved in extra-curricular activities performed better in school compared to students who were not involved in such activities. Typically, sponsors of these activities took a vested interest in the students not only in the extra-curricular activities such as band, football, baseball, volleyball or cheerleading, but also in the classrooms. These sponsors would form partnerships with the teachers and parents of the students.

When the student's performance was not up to par, the teachers would inform the sponsors and subsequently the students would get reprimanded in practices or games to reinforce academic excellence. Sponsors would also inform the parents on how their children were performing in the extra-curricular activities and the classrooms. This would happen at the activity practices, events or through other communication channels. Thus, these students became fully aware of the partnerships formed with their sponsors, teachers and parents and realized there was little or no excuse for misbehaving academically or socially in school.

Just like other organizations, the school system has to find its niche for continuous improvement in meeting the needs of students. Research has proven that schools that employ highly qualified teachers and school leaders, offer a rigorous curriculum, focus on teaching and learning and the like lead to educational achievement. Research also has proven that students who participate in extra-curricular activities at schools improve their academics, attendance and behavior and subsequently become motivated to pursue higher education. With the use of a large sample size on a national level, the NIAAA research adds to the existing knowledge that there is a positive correlation between athletic involvement and academic success.

What makes DISD's School for the Talented and Gifted the top in the nation?

Dynasties are rare yet they exist in arenas such as politics, sports and companies. Some people say that the Bushes and Kennedys resembled a dynasty in politics. The Dallas Cowboys and San Francisco 49ers of earlier years symbolized a dynasty in sports and companies such as Walt Disney and Walmart have provided excellent years of service.

However, little is written about high performing schools that consistently prepare students for college and careers in a global and competitive workforce. To gain an understanding of the commitment and characteristics of high performing schools, the critical question to be asked is: What makes Dallas Independent School District's School for the Talented and Gifted the top in the nation for two consecutive years?

The School for the Talented and Gifted (TAG) places emphasis on the advanced placement curriculum requiring its students to take a minimum of 11 advanced placement courses for graduation. With an enrollment of 240 high school students (43 percent White, 30 percent Hispanic, 17 percent African-American, 11 percent Asian and 29 percent eligible for free or reduced lunch), TAG affords its students the opportunity for field research through partnerships with local universities, enroll in mini-courses such as ballroom dancing during interim terms and take electives such as web mastery.

With college-level course work being the benchmark, the school achieved 100 percent proficiency on its state test for reading and mathematics, as well as 100 percent proficiency for college readiness as measured by student participation rates in advanced placement and international baccalaureate exams, as well as pass rates on the exams.

The *U.S. World and News Report* recognizes America's best high schools based on students' performance on the state reading and mathematics exams, college readiness index-based participation rates in advanced placement and international baccalaureate courses, as well as the performance of students on the national exams. *U.S. News* also takes in consideration of those schools that effectively meet the needs of their students or successfully serve all of them well regardless of their socio-economic status. Based on *U.S. News* criteria, TAG became the top school in the nation for two consecutive years. This school was selected from 22,000 public schools covering 49 states including the District of Columbia.

Principal Michael Satarino of the School for the Talented and Gifted said, "It is both humbling and gratifying to be named the top school in the nation. It is gratifying because it allows our incredible teachers, students and parents to receive recognition for the passion they bring to their educational ministry at TAG every day."

It is stimulating to learn of a high performing public school that consistently prepares students for college and careers in a global and competitive workforce. The School for the Talented and Gifted is an excellent model for other schools to benchmark and emulate.

How can schools improve educational opportunities for military children?

Approximately 1.25 million military children in the U.S. are school age and nearly 80 percent of them attend public schools throughout the nation. Five hundred thousand military children move six to nine times during their K-12 years, according to the Military Child Education Coalition. Some have difficulties transitioning socially and academically due to constant deployments of one or both of their parents. So the critical questions to be asked are: How can schools improve educational opportunities for military children? What is the Department of Defense Educational Activity (DoDEA)? How does Fort Huachuca Schools (FHS) participate in the DoDEA grant program? What are some of the successes at FHS?

While the majority of military families reside on or near a military installation in the U.S. and some of them are stationed in overseas locations, the Department of Defense Educational Activity offers a grant program to Local Educational Agencies with military children. The program is designed to (1) promote student achievement in the core curricular areas; (2) ease the challenges that military students face due to transitions and deployments; (3) support the unique social and emotional needs of military students; (4) promote distance learning opportunities; (5) improve educator professional development; (6) enhance and integrate technology and (6) encourage parental involvement. DoDEA has awarded nearly $200 million in grants to over 180 military-connected school districts since 2008.

One school district that is a participant of the DoDEA grant program is Fort Huachuca Schools (FHS). FHS is led by superintendent Dr. Ronda Frueauff. She has been a superintendent for 19 years in three different school systems in Arizona and Ohio, and superintendent at FHS for the past eight years. According to former Superintendent, Dr. Frueauff, FHS is a K-8 Arizona public school system located on the Fort Huachuca Military Post which is a military intelligence and communication training center. The system is comprised of three schools that were built in the past eight years with a student enrollment of 1100 who predominantly reside on the army post. On the average, FHS has an attrition rate of 60 percent due to the deployment and duty reassignments of military dependents throughout the school year. Soldiers are assigned to Fort Huachuca a minimum of six months to three years depending upon the specialty of the soldiers.

FHS is in its second year of the three-year grant program funded by the DoDEA. The district's program focuses on 21st Century Skills, projects-based and inquiry learning with an emphasis on Science, Technology, Engineering and Mathematics. The program spans all schools K-8. The intent is to promote students with a comprehensive college and career ready education that will allow them to be successful in any high school program, says Frueauff.

Additionally, Frueauff discusses the type of curriculum and technology integration used at FHS. She says that the school district incorporates the Technology Integration Matrix (AZ K-12 Center) and the STEM Quality Framework (Washington STEM and Dayton Regional STEM Center) to guide the integration process for the projects-based, technology-enhanced instructional programs at each school. Teachers and students at each school site are supported by a technology integration specialist who provides quality professional development and coaching for all staff members. Teachers are also evaluated utilizing the Stronge Evaluation Model developed by James H. Stronge from Virginia.

In addition to the typical sports, choral music and band programs, FHS sponsors extracurricular programs such as Future Cities, Lego League, computer programming, Technology Experts, Step It Up Club, Magellan Running Club, Drama Club, virtual 3-D modeling, Knowledge Bowl, Flute Club and Youth Engineering and Science Competitions. With all of the academic and support programs at FHS and a very active Parent Teacher Organization at each of its schools, 96 percent of the students are prepared for the next grade level. Students score from 70 percent proficient to 95 percent proficient on Arizona state assessments in Reading, Writing, Mathematics and Science, says Frueauff.

Why did Putnam County School District implement the Sixth Grade Center?

School districts have implemented different grade configurations such as K-5, K-6, 6-8, 7-8 or 9-12 to accommodate the academic and social needs of students. Many factors should be considered when school districts determine the appropriate grade configurations for their school communities. This might include the impact on parent involvement and other schools, the design of the school building, the student population, the student socioeconomic background, the transportation cost and the school districts' expectations for student achievement. For this feature, the critical questions to be asked are: Why did Putnam County School District (PCSD) implement the Sixth Grade Center? What is unique about the curriculum for the Sixth Grade Center? What advice does Superintendent Phyllis Criswell give to superintendents for implementing a Six Grade Center?

Putnam County School District is located in Palatka, Florida. It operates on a budget of $86 million with a teaching staff of 720 and 11,039 students occupying 21 schools. In PCSD, 55 percent of the students are White, 25 percent African-American, 16 percent Hispanic, 3.5 percent multi-racial, .6 percent Asian, .3 percent Indian and .09 percent Hawaiian. Of the student population, 78 percent are on free and/or reduced lunch. PCSD is led by Superintendent Phyllis Criswell who has been with the district in different roles for 29 years. In her first year as superintendent, Criswell implemented the Cambridge Program (K-9th grade) and the Six Grade Center. Following is an excerpt of Criswell's description of the Sixth Grade Center:

Implementation of Six Grade Center

We have the greatest number of dropouts in the ninth grade, and that starts in sixth grade. We had to do something to reduce the dropout rate. Our students come from the elementary (K-5) where they had a very supervised environment with one teacher the entire day, to a middle school (6-8) of several teachers, where they are still immature and yet have a great deal more responsibility placed on them. It is very difficult for many of our children who came out of fifth grade coupled with a fifth grade mentality to be placed into six classes for 50 minutes and expected to keep up with their homework and assignments. They needed a little more time to slow down and learn the process and let their mind and body catch up on what we are trying to do with them academically.

My thought was that there are many other districts in the state and nation that have used Sixth Grade Centers, and we had never implemented that program in Putnam County School District. We can't do it county-wide because we are too large of a county. We were able to do it in the Palatka area because five of our 10 elementary schools are in the Palatka community. We had two middle schools in Palatka. We converted those schools to a seventh and eighth grade middle school, and a sixth grade center. Our five elementary schools now feed into the Six Grade Center.

The Six Grade Center gives students another year to mature. It gives them the opportunity to really work on their academics to prepare for middle school, as well as their social and emotional well-being. Additionally, the Six Grade Center gives us just that one grade to concentrate on so we can do more unique programs for the children. For example, we have a program called Creating Lasting Families Connections to address bullying with our students and particularly teach them: how not to be a bully, how to recognize a bully, how to deal with bullying, and how to avoid bullying. We are developing full-six week programs, with our six graders, to teach them about manners, careers, test-taking, life-skills and many other fun, meaningful and unique activities.

Uniqueness of Curriculum

The unique part about the curriculum is that we are using block scheduling, and our teachers all know that they are teachers of reading. Reading is the one thing our students need to be successful. So whether our teachers are teaching social studies, science or math, they will concentrate on reading in their respective subject or content areas to ensure that students understand how to read and learn the vocabulary for those areas. Instead of students changing classes five or six times a day, through block scheduling, they are changing classes only three times a day. Their classes are blocked so that they have additional time in those classes to improve academically and eliminate unnecessary time in the hallways where they tend to get in trouble. We really think this will make a difference as they move forward to middle school. These students don't have to worry about seventh and eighth graders picking on them. In fact, they are all six graders and all equal to each other at this point. We just feel this will give them an added advantage that they have not had previously.

Because the principal and assistant principal at the Six Grade Center and seventh and eighth grade middle school are working together, this will also make a smooth transition from the center to the middle school. Palatka High School, where these students will ultimately attend, the teachers are really happy about the change because they said previously, the kids from the two middle schools had a rivalry and when they came to high school, the rivalry would carry over to the high school and create discipline problems there. This center will eliminate that problem because there are no longer two middle schools. With the new design, we now have a Six Grade Center and a seventh and eighth grade middle school allowing a better flow from elementary to middle to high school, enabling students to become acquainted with each other and eliminating the rivalry between schools and subsequently discipline problems. In addition to K-5, we also have a Cambridge Program for 6-9 providing a rigorous internationally recognized pre-university curriculum that gives students a broad, balanced preparation for college honors-degree programs.

Advice to Superintendents

For implementing any program, you really need to look at the staff that you have. Do you have people who have the leadership, knowledge, skills and abilities to implement a Six Grade Center or any program you want to start? Do you feel comfortable and confident in their leadership, knowledge, skills and abilities? If yes, I would say go forward with a Six Grade Center because it really starts with the credentials of your staff. If you have people who are good leaders and can implement the program effectively, then certainly it is good to make a change. Change is not always easy for people but it often can be just what you need in order to be more successful with your students. Every decision or plan you make should be about the students, not about the adults. In Putnam, we just felt that this was the best thing we could do for our six graders in order to increase their academic achievement and reduce our dropout rate.

We did have some parents at the beginning who were not happy about the program and did not think it would work. They were not happy we were sending the seventh and eighth graders from one middle school to the other middle school. Their fears were alleviated the first week of school since it worked beautifully. The children worked well together at the seventh and eighth grade school because of the teachers. We have a lot of good teachers who are used to working with seventh and eighth grade students and they said even the first day of school, you could not tell one middle school from another. The teachers had lots of activities for students to get to know each other and their new school. We had absolutely no problems.

Regarding School Systems

How can schools prepare students for a 21st Century Workforce?

Candice Glover became the 2013 American Idol winner after pursuing her dream three times. By winning this competition, Candice is set to become an accomplished recording artist, star in movies and possibly win a Grammy. Just as American Idol prepares young people for a career in the entertainment industry, schools ultimately have the job of preparing students for the workforce. Therefore, the critical questions to be asked are: How can schools prepare students for a 21st century workforce? What are the 16 national career clusters delineated by the U.S. Department of Education? What is a potential path of study for ninth graders? What is a model Career and Technical Education program?

With a high demand for a rigorous curriculum aligned with a 21st century workforce, public school students in many states are participating in a Career Technical Education (CTE) program that allow students to choose a potential job to pursue or path of study in one of the 16 national career clusters of the U.S. Department of Education. These career clusters which have defined occupations under each area include (1) agriculture, food and natural resources, (2) audio/visual technology and communications, (3) architecture and construction, (4) business, management and administration, (5) education and training, (6) finance, (7) government and public administration, (8) health science, (9) hospitality and tourism, (10) human services, (11) information technology, (12) manufacturing, (13) marketing, sales and science, (14) public safety and security, (15) science, technology, engineering and mathematics and (16) transportation, distribution and logistics.

According to Finlayson (2009), the Tennessee Department of Education required all students in the ninth grade to choose a career path of study including academic, technical and dual. A ninth grade student on the "academic path must have one fine art credit and two foreign language credits in addition to the required credits for graduation; a student on the technical path must have four credits in one technical area in addition to the required credits for graduation; and a student on the dual path must have both the four technical credits in one area and the additional fine art and foreign language credits." The understanding is that students' exposure to a wide range of choices will provide additional options for pursuing college and careers.

Project Lead the Way (PLTW) is an example of a Career Technical Education program. While initially launched in 12 New York high schools in the late 1990s and currently in over 3500 high schools nationwide, PLTW is a pathway to engineering that uses a rigorous curriculum through a four-year sequence of courses. Before moving to more specialized options such as architecture, biotechnical and civil engineering, students complete the necessary foundation courses such as introduction to engineering design and principles of engineering. The program ends with a capstone course in engineering design and development. Students work in teams to research and develop a solution to an open-ended engineering problem according to research.

To grade schools on its effectiveness of preparing students for college and career readiness, the State of Georgia in 2012 implemented a College and Career Ready Performance Index (CCRPI) to ensure that all students graduate from high school with both rigorous content knowledge and the ability to apply that knowledge for college-level work and careers. While the CCRPI in Georgia replaces the No Child Left Behind Act, it remains to be seen the effectiveness of this model.

Thus, just as American Idol has it forum to find the best singers and prepare them for a career in entertainment, public schools can use the 16 national career clusters as a framework to prepare students for careers in a plethora of occupations in line with the demands for a 21st century economy.

How can schools use content marketing to promote their programs and services?

Before the information age, businesses marketed their brands through mediums such as television, radio and print. With the change in times, the traditional approaches to marketing are outdated. Consumers pay less attention to commercials and even utilize technology such as TIVO to record their favorite programs allowing them to skip the commercials for their convenience. To be competitive in a social networking era, businesses must now use content marketing to attract consumers. With school budgets being tight and funding predicated on student enrollment, schools must also find innovative ways to promote their programs and services, as well as maintain their bottom line. So the critical questions to be asked are: How can schools use a content marketing approach to promote their programs and services?

According to the Content Marketing Institute, content marketing is designed to "create and share relevant and valuable content to attract, acquire and engage a clearly defined target audience with the goal of driving profitable customer action." The motivation behind content marketing is the belief that customers will purchase our products or rewards us their business and loyalty if we deliver consistent and relevant information to them.

In a Content Marketing Seminar, Rachel O'Connell, director of the online marketing company, Constant Contact talked about the future of content marketing. O'Connell says that in the past from a content marketing standpoint, there were limited communication channels and thus, the organization was able to control the information about its brand. In a social media era, consumers can learn about your brand from various sources. And, consumers trust and value more of the information about the brand that is coming from their friends and colleagues than from the actual organization. To meet the challenges of this new marketplace in attracting customers to your business, firm or school, O'Connell recommends that organizational leaders consider the following when using content marketing: (1) be where they are; (2) find multiple ways to tell your story and (3) get out of the spotlight.

"To be where your customers are," O'Connell suggests that you promote your programs and services through all facets of social media. This includes Facebook, Twitter, Google, Linkedin, YouTube, Pinterest etc. In doing so, O'Connell emphasizes the importance of being real, human and responsive to your audience for effectiveness. From a K-12 perspective, schools should use a social media strategy to market their academic and extra-curricular programs to parents especially since social media is prevalent among all age groups. The adage that says, "If you can't beat them, then join them," applies to the use of the social media to promote programs and services in schools.

In O'Connell's second illustration, "find multiple ways to tell a story," she suggests that organizations promote their programs and services through different communication mediums. For a school that is in compliance with its district for having permission to use photos or video of children, this might encompass advertising a special student program on the school's Facebook site by including a video clip, pictures or photo albums of students performing in a school play. This gives the audience an opportunity to learn about an event or service in an engaging manner. Instead of thinking what do I need to tell consumers, the adage is, what can I show them. O'Connell says that you should let your content be transparent so that it entices people to act. This is so important because students enjoy seeing their peers in the limelight and simulating the experiences they may have in the same setting.

O'Connell's third example for attracting consumers to your business, firm or school is to "get out of the spotlight." This means, looking for opportunities for reliable sources to share their experiences with your brand. When others have good experiences with your brand, they are willing to tell your story which means the news travels to other potential audiences. For a school, one example of this might include sharing the success of the organization with local realtors and businesses. Thus, these entities become reliable sources that can express positive experiences with potential parents.

In times of a tight fiscal budget combined with funding being tied to student enrollment, school must employ creative approaches, "outside the box" thinking to promote their programs and services to parents. Content marketing is an approach that businesses use to engage consumers about their products and services. These same approaches have relevancy for schools as we grapple with ways to keep students and parents informed about the services and programs that are available to educate our children. We encourage schools to use these innovative strategies to entice their current and potential stakeholders and maintain good business relationships with them.

How can school districts create a culture of excellence for all students, staff and families?

For our students to develop 21st century skills such as critical thinking, problem solving and communication germane to a global and competitive workforce, education must be our top priority. While attending the 2013 National Conference on Education in Los Angeles, superintendents across the nation were welcomed with talented speakers to network and learn best practices critical to the sustainability and vitality of the education profession. Despite tough economic times, the critical questions to be asked are: How can school districts create a culture of excellence for all students, staff and families? How can they transform schools for improvement?

Deborah S. Delisle, Assistant Secretary for the Office of Elementary and Secondary Education for the U. S. Department of Education, was one of the dynamic speakers for the conference. She gave personal and professional recommendations for school districts to create a culture of excellence for all students, staff and families in order to transform schools for improvement. Delisle told the superintendents that her father was her greatest teacher who instilled the value in her as a child that "You can be anything you want, if you care enough." Consequently, she has held on to this belief and made it an integral part of her personal and professional life.

Delisle's message was passionate and compelling for superintendents to consider transforming their schools through telling students what we value, predict what students need for their future, afford students hope and a reason to report to school daily since many of them come to school bored and tired due to challenging and stressful situations at home. Delisle said students don't care about whether we are opponents or proponents of the Democratic or Republican party. We must create a positive climate that gives students hope for the next day.

Just as we create a culture of excellence for students, Delisle said we must do the same for staff and families. She discussed the need for school districts to look at their support structure or ways to show appreciation for staff that change teaching and administrative positions throughout their careers, and think critically about how they engage or welcome parents to the school. She cautioned educators to be aware of intention and the conflicting messages we may send. She provided the example of a school that indicated it has an open door policy although there was a sign at the school that said family hours are from 3-4 p.m., which could cause a major issue for working families.

Delisle believes "the primary aim of education is not to enable students to do well in school, but to help them do well in the lives they lead outside of school now and in the future." She explained that school districts must identify ways to personalize education in an effort to get to know their students. She said that surveys can be a way to assess what families and students think about their schools but the data collected has to be acted upon. She gave an example of how one school accepted the feedback of students and, subsequently, their scores improved. She said it is amazing what happens when teachers sincerely invest their hearts in children. Improvement can happen consistently in schools. However, Delisle stated that "unless we unlearn some of our traditional practices, we will never get beyond an improvement mindset."

Additionally, Delisle discussed the need for school districts to employ a strategic transformation mindset to "prepare children of today for a world that has yet to be created, for jobs yet to be invented and for technologies yet undreamed." She explained a scenario in her role as associate superintendent in Cleveland where an Advanced Placement program was costing the district one million dollars each year although the program was counter-productive due to an insufficient number of students in the program. She advised superintendents in similar situations to strategically rethink the value of the program rather than maintain the status quo. In our jobs, "sometimes our behaviors become rote and predictable which does not lead to transformative and supportive systems," noted Delisle.

Delisle said that when you enter a school, you are able to determine immediately the climate and make a decision to enroll or not enroll your child in the school. The culture tells everything. To improve the culture, "We should focus on what the teachers should be doing instead of what the students are doing." In other words, what type of lesson did the teachers develop to foster learning? Similarly, we should focus on how the teachers are responding to the principals. Are principals just keeping track of the number of classroom walkthroughs or providing relevant feedback to the lessons with the teachers? Performance reviews should be about the practices that prepare students for 21st century skills. Delisle said, superintendents have to model the kinds of meetings, observations and expectations they want their principals to have with the teachers and other staff. They must establish the non-negotiables. Everyone in the building including the secretary must be held accountable to change the culture and, subsequently, improve the learning environment. The way the secretary answers the telephone even sends a message about the culture.

Culture is essential to the success of schools according to Delisle. She said that when looking at the culture of the school, we should ask questions such as, "What do we see? What do we hear staff members saying? What does the physical environment look like? How are problems resolved? What are our stakeholders saying about us? What is the energy level? Is the environment conducive to working collaboratively?"

Delisle ended her presentation by asking administrators the following questions: "Are you preparing our students for their future? To what extent do your students have opportunities to engage in interdisciplinary studies, blended learning, guided inquiry, projects that cross times zones, career exploration, mentorships and internships." She noted that "higher performing districts tend to be led by staff that communicate a strong belief in the capacity of principals and teachers to improve the quality of teaching and learning and in the district's capacity to develop the organizational conditions needed for that to happen."

While school districts are faced with a plethora of challenges, Delisle emphasized that networking is critical. "Every state is different, kids are different" but we all have the same goal to educate our students. The National Conference on Education affords superintendents and other school leaders to talk to each other about educational issues and solutions for creating viable school cultures conducive to learning. According to Delisle, "Our students are depending upon us to create a culture of excellence for all of them. Tomorrow is too late."

How did Douglas County School District avoid a budget cut?

While many school districts are struggling to balance their operating budget, one school district in Colorado was able to avoid budget cuts for the 2013-2014 school year entirely. Given this economic environment, the questions to be asked are: How did Douglas County School District (DCSD) avoid a budget cut for the 2013-2014 school year? What advice does Dr. Elizabeth Fagen give to superintendents for balancing the budget? How did DCSD look closely at all contracts for reallocation possibilities? How does being transparent promote the good of DCSD?

Douglas County School District is located in Castle Rock, Colorado south of Denver. With a teaching staff of 6,400, DCSD is the third largest school district in Colorado serving over 64,000 students in approximately 80 schools. In 2011, DCSD was confronted with a budget deficit of $18 million. DCSD developed a budget package with three goals in mind: to prepare every student to compete on the world stage for any college or career of their choice; improve the quality of life for employees and continue to improve the fiscal health of the district.

Under the leadership of Superintendent Dr. Elizabeth Fagen, DCSD will have no budget cuts for the 2013-14 school year. As reported in the district's November 2012 press release, Fagen said, "We have reviewed the state revenue forecast, we have reviewed the Governor's budget proposal and we have reviewed possible increased cost in the district for next year – like PERA, health insurance premiums and fuel costs – and we have determined that given the stability and excellent fiscal health of our budget, we will be making no budget reductions for next year."

With such a remarkable accomplishment during the time of a stiff economy, I asked Fagen to elaborate further on DCSD's budgetary process and sustainability. Particularly, I asked her what advice she would give to superintendents for balancing the budget, how did DCSD look closely at all contracts for reallocation possibilities and how does being transparent promote the good of DCSD? An excerpt of Fagen's responses follows:

Advice to Superintendents:

I am a superintendent who really believes that every district is unique. Every school or community is unique. My position is that when you come into a new district, you have to really get to know the district, its budget, all of its line items and all of its contractual obligations. Then, you have to match those things to the vision, priorities and mission of the district. You have to make sure that everything is aligned. What works in Douglas County may or may not work in another school district.

I think every superintendent needs to be hands-on with his or her budget (I am). The superintendent has to work very hard to ensure that he or she is spending the district's dollars exactly the way the superintendent would want someone to spend his or her own money. When I make decisions about how we spend money, I am always thinking about is this best for students? Is this aligned with the vision we have for our school district? Are we being as efficient with our dollars as we can so that our tax payers will see that we are very good steward of those dollars? I think those are three important filters.

Before the recession, one thing that happened in education is that we continued to add things to the budget. However, it seems like we didn't spend enough time reviewing what we have and don't need to do anymore. In DCSD, we have gone to considerable length to make sure that we are as efficient and excellent as possible while maintaining our focus on students. We stopped doing things that no longer makes sense. To do such, you have to thoroughly review all of your spending for opportunities before just adding.

Contracts Reallocation Possibilities:

When we looked at our DCSD budget, we realized that our employees had been on a four-year pay freeze; and there were conversations about doing furlough days prior to my arrival. In going through all of our budgetary contracts, we realized that we had this program called extended service severance (ESS). We were paying new teachers coming into the district an annual salary of approximately $34,000. At the same time, we were paying retiring teachers who were making far bigger salaries an average of $40,000 dollars in one final check to leave. This accounted for about two point two million dollars in our budget every year, and we needed over two point eight million to give our staff a one percent raise. We made the hard decision to phase out the severance program because this was not our teachers' pension plan. It had only been around since 2009. More importantly, we already pay about 16 percent each year to PERA – Public Employee Retirement Association in Colorado for all DCSD employees. After phasing out the ESS program, we gave everybody in the district the one percent raise although we had no new money from the state. This is just one example of how we looked at a particular line item, determined where we could save money and reapplied the money to provide a raise for employees.

In another example, we worked really hard to save money in utilities and other costs. As a district including the teamwork of those involved in our "sustainability initiative," DCSD saved over $14,000,000 in six years. Electrical use per square foot dropped over 20 percent. Consequently, we gave our employees a two percent stipend or one-time compensation in addition to the one percent raise generated from the phase out of the ESS. When most districts were cutting things and not giving employees anything, we scrutinized our budget and reallocated dollars in ways that made sense; and actually gave one of the largest increases on the Front Range during one of the worst fiscal years we have ever had.

Being Transparent:

When coming into a new district, you have to make some changes and at the same time build trust, integrity and credibility. Having over 6,500 employees, 64,000 students and 100,000 parents such as DCSD, one of the ways you can build trust and credibility is by being transparent. Although you can not sit down at the table and have coffee with every person, you can encourage everyone in your district to look at your website, download your app, listen to your radio show, watch

DCSD TV, and participate in telephone town halls. In DCSD, every stakeholder is able to review our budget on the website, watch emailed videos of me and my CFO explaining it, ask questions about it during telephone town halls, hear about it on the radio, and more. We really work hard to be transparent through our website and many other communication tools. In fact, our community relations team posts three minute videos on the website that provides a cursory view of all new programs, services and activities in the district so people do not have to read lengthy documents if that is their preference. On the other hand, we post many lengthy documents also for those who really enjoy digging into the information and data.

Is it time to bail out U.S. school districts?

The domino theory suggests that if the U.S. government bails out one organization in dire financial crisis, then it should be prepared to bail out another organization of similar circumstances. Using taxpayers' money, the U.S. government appropriated $700 billion to bail out financial systems such as banks through the Emergency Economic Stabilization Act of 2008. Similarly, the federal government spent $24.9 billion in 2009 to bail out General Motors and Chrysler from layoffs and deterioration.

So the question to be asked is: Is it time to bail out U.S. school districts? School districts nationwide are faced with substantial cutbacks or shortfalls due to an unstable and uncertain economy. Similar to the banking and auto industries, school districts are in need of financial support from the U.S. government to stabilize themselves from excessive layoffs of employees and, subsequently, destruction.

On Feb. 28, 2012, for example, the San Francisco Board of Education approved preliminary layoff notices for over 485 full-time positions in San Francisco Unified School District (SFUSD). SFUSD has about 8,000 employees and serves 56,000 pre-kindergarten through 12th grade students. The proposed layoffs represent approximately 106 paraprofessionals, 123 administrators and 245 instructional services including teachers, counselors and other employees.

These projections are based on California Governor Jerry Brown's proposed budget deficit of $83.3 million in the event his tax proposal of $119.4 million does not pass for the next two years. According to Superintendent Carlos Garcia,

SFUSD is "facing another year of devastating budget cuts from the state. Though we wish we didn't have to layoff any employee, we must do what is right for the children in our highest need schools and communities."

SFUSD's preliminary layoff notices are mandatory for all certified employees by March 15 of each year. During the past two school years, all employees in SFUSD took four furlough days to minimize layoffs. The SFUSD is seeking the continuation of furlough days for an additional two years to offset costs and, subsequently, reserve positions. However, the district is confronted with the uncertainty of the state's budget and other factors to maintain a balanced budget with existing employees. It is forced to rely on the proposed cuts by the state, issue final layoff notices to employees by May and submit its budget to the state by July 1, according to the school system.

In Oakland United School District - 2012, the school board approved the closing of five elementary schools located in the predominantly Latino, African-American and Southeast Asian communities; whereby the wealthier communities did not face school closures, according to the Oakland Tribune. An Occupy Hood group along with concerned parents and other community officials requested the school board find a way to bailout these schools in the same way as the banks. This group expressed that its taxpayer dollars have been funneled to prisons and financial systems instead of schools.

In Philadelphia, the message of a school district bailout was heard "loud and clear." The Chester Upland School District was unable to meet its one million payroll and expected to have a $20 million deficit by the end of the school year. Consequently, a judge ordered the state to give the district a 3.2 million advancement to pay its bills, according to the Philadelphia Inquirer. School officials complained that the state appropriate funds illegally to support charter schools. However, state officials noted that they fund schools by law based on student enrollment.

According to the Center of Budget and Policy Priorities (CBPP), 31 U.S. states have projected or addressed budget shortfalls of 55 billion for the 2013 fiscal year. Among these states, California, Florida and Pennsylvania estimated a total shortfall of $16.2 billion, $1 billion and $540 million respectively. When states are faced with budget shortfalls during an economic downturn, spending cuts are problematic.

These cuts may encompass layoffs of employees, cancellation of contracts with vendors, elimination of companies that provide direct services and postponement of benefit payments to individuals. Consequently, this creates a domino effect in that employees and employers have less capital to spend on products and goods to support the economy. So raising taxes and enacting strategic cuts are essential to address state budget gaps and maintain important services "while minimizing harmful effects of the economy," according to CBPP.

The Golden Rule reminds us to "do unto others as you would have them to do unto you." When the automotive and financial industries were struggling to balance their budgets, the U.S. government found a way to support them through an emergency bailout initiative. This was done at the expense of taxpayers with the understanding that there would be a return on investment and, also, these organizations would repay their debts to the federal government. Whether or not the loans have been repaid to the government, school districts are faced with a financial hardship placing their students' education in jeopardy. Contrary to popular beliefs, the domino theory suggests: It is time to bail out U.S. school districts.

What is replacing the No Child Left Behind law in Georgia?

According to The New York Times, approximately 38,000 of the nation's 100,000 public schools did not meet their No Child Left Behind (NCLB) testing targets in 2010 and about half as many schools did not meet their targets in 2011. As a result, the U.S. Department of Education in the fall of 2011 challenged state education agencies to request flexibility from the federal No Child Left Behind law. Georgia was one of eleven state agencies that filed and received approval from the NCLB through an application process.

In the application, state agencies were to provide an intervention utilizing multiple measures to assess the effectiveness of schools rather adopt a one-size-fits all remedy of the NCLB/Adequate Yearly Progress (AYP) measurement. So, the critical questions to be asked are: What is replacing the No Child Left Behind law in Georgia? How does the College and Career Ready Performance Index (CCRPI) work? What does College and Career readiness mean? What are the results of Georgia schools from the CCRPI?

Georgia's State School Superintendent Dr. John Barge released the new accountability system called the Georgia College and Career Ready Performance Index in May of 2013. CCRPI measures schools and school districts on an easy-to-understand scale. The index is designed to help parents and the community better understand how schools are performing in a more comprehensive manner than the pass or fail system under the AYP. Specifically, each school receives a score or grade ranging from 0 to 100, similar to a student classroom grade.

A school is scored using the ratings: achievement, progress and achievement gap with possible points of 70, 15 and 15 respectively. A school can be eligible for a possible 10 "challenge points" if it has a significant number of economically disadvantaged students, English Learner students and Students with Disabilities meeting expectations. Also, a school can receive points for going beyond the targets of the CCRPI by challenging students to exceed expectations and participate in college and career readiness programs. College and Career Readiness means that all students graduate from high school with both rigorous content knowledge and the ability to apply that knowledge for college-level work and careers.

Based on data from the 2011-2012 school year, the average score for Georgia's elementary schools is 83.4, middle schools is 81.4 and high schools is 72.6. Factors for scoring high school is different for elementary and middle schools. The graduation rate is a part of the scoring, and it is calculated based on students completing high school (ninth through twelfth grade) within four years. Unlike the NCLB, the index gives the state more autonomy in measuring the effectiveness of its schools, eliminates the annual measurable objectives, provides credits or points for each indicator (such as achievement progress) and replaces the needs improvement schools with priority and focus schools. According to Superintendent Barge, "I am very pleased that we now have a school improvement measure as in-depth as the College and Career Ready Performance Index. We are no longer bound by the narrow definitions of success found in the Adequate Yearly Progress measurement. Holding schools accountable and rewarding them for the work they do in all subjects and with all students is critical in preparing our students to be college and career ready. The index effectively measures how schools prepare our students for success."

What schools are honorees of the 2013 Green Ribbon Schools?

"Going green" is changing the way we live, work and act for the safety and benefit of our natural resources. As such, we are carpooling, recycling and reusing products to be more environmentally friendly. With the U.S. Department of Education's implementation of a recognition award for K-12 schools that focus on green initiatives, the critical questions to be asked are: What schools are honorees of the 2013 U.S. Department of Education Green Ribbon Schools? What are some best practices exemplified by these schools?

In its second year of implementation, the U.S. Department of Education Green Ribbon Schools (ED-GRS) recognition honors schools that are exemplary in reducing environmental impact and costs; improving the health and wellness of students and staff and providing effective environmental and sustainability education, which incorporates STEM, civic skills and green career pathways.

In 2013, a total of 64 schools (54 public and 10 private) were announced winners on Earth Day, April 22. These honorees represented 29 states and the District of Columbia with California, Pennsylvania, Washington and Wisconsin having the most honorees. More than half of the honorees educate underserved student populations, and 40 percent of the populations are eligible for free and reduced lunch.

According to Secretary of Education Arne Duncan, "The honorees are modeling a comprehensive approach to being green. They are demonstrating ways schools can simultaneously cut costs; improve health, performance and equity; and provide an education geared toward the jobs of the future. In fact, the selected districts are saving millions of dollars as a result of their greening efforts. And the great thing is that the resources these honorees are using are available for free to all schools."

As a model for other schools, the following provides an excerpt of two honorees' initiatives: Driftwood Middle School in Hollywood, Florida and Ford Elementary School in Acworth, Georgia.

Driftwood Middle School:

Across the board, green practices have led to improved science scores, reduced environmental costs and impacts, and more balanced diets at Florida's Driftwood Middle School Academy of Health and Wellness, where 73 percent of the students are eligible for free or reduced rate lunches. Driftwood's conservation efforts began in 2008 with the launch of its energy reduction challenge, "How Low Can You Go?" Since then, students and teachers have used multiple creative means to effectively reduce its carbon footprint.

To encourage teachers to turn off lights after school hours, Green Team students left painted paw prints stating "You've been chilled!" on the classroom doors of those who had not. As a result, Greenhouse Gas emissions dropped 23 percent. Water use dramatically dropped by 38 percent -- with 70 percent of the school's outdoor campus landscaped with native plants that thrive on natural rainfall. Forty-five percent of campus-generated waste is recycled, with special needs students taking the lead in collecting bottles and cans. The drama club won the Broward County Public Broadcasting Announcement Video Contest with its "Recycle, Reduce, and Reuse" video.

Ford Elementary School:

Ford Elementary School sits amid more than 20 acres and uses more than 60 percent of the grounds for environmental education and habitat protection. Built in 1991, Ford Elementary was designed to accommodate 900 students, but within three years needed to educate more than 1700 students. Within its first year,

Ford became a National Wildlife Federation Certified Schoolyard Habitat. After additional schools were built to relieve overcrowding, Ford became proactive in reclaiming its native habitats.

During the summer of 2013, Ford Elementary will undergo its first extensive renovation since the building was constructed. Several energy saving projects will reduce environmental impact and improve the health and safety of students, staff and the community. Once the project is complete, it will be eligible to apply for the EPA's ENERGY STAR certification. Highlights of the project include a new HVAC system and occupancy sensors in each room to more effectively regulate energy usage. At the conclusion of the project, Ford expects its energy efficiency to increase from approximately 80 percent to over 92 percent.

How can school districts benefit from a zero-based budgeting model?

People work for 30 plus years to retire and then expect a return on their time investment. This might include a combination of savings, pensions, annuities, royalties and social security. In a stiff economy, school districts are faced with budgetary shortfalls. They are looking for innovative and efficient ways to improve student achievement while managing tight budgets.

So the questions to be asked: How can school districts benefit from a zero-based budgeting model? How should the zero-based budgeting model be created to show a return on investment? How does the expenditure budget differ from the zero-based budgeting model?

According to research, zero-based budgeting is defined as a method whereby each manager's operating budget must be justified from zero for all existing and newly requested programs. This process is conducted each fiscal year compared to budgetary decisions being based on previous year's funding level.

To get a better understanding of zero-based budgeting model, I interviewed Superintendent Kelt Cooper of Del Rio Consolidated Independent School District in Del Rio, Texas. As superintendent with experience in multiple school districts, Cooper says that the zero-based budgeting model "analyzes human materials and data to determine if there is value" in activities being funded. He believes that all activities must have a purpose and desired outcome. School leaders must be able to defend their reasons for spending. They must measure the effectiveness of the activities to determine if there is a return on investment.

In order to show a return on investment, Cooper says that the zero-based budgeting model must critically analyze whether the activities being conducted are meeting their intended objective in the most efficient way. He explained that many schools organize staff development activities just for the sake of having activities to satisfy federal guidelines. Cooper provided an example where a school district spent almost $15,000 to promote a district-wide parental involvement activity at a community civic center, however, less than 20 percent of the parent population attended the event. In addition, the activity was a duplicate to an open house activity meaning the budget could have been spent in some other capacity and at a cheaper cost. In a similar case example, Cooper talked about a Quilting Club that had a sizeable stipend and functioned for eight years without any students. The return on investment was nil yet the principal was maintaining the program on the books and transferring the funds to his student activity account.

Through the zero-based budgeting model, Cooper says that there are baseline facts you cannot ignore, such as teachers' contracts. However, he believes that you still can look at efficient ways to budget activities to meet the needs of the organization.

When newly appointed Superintendent Dr. Cheryl Atkinson of DeKalb County School System was questioned about how she would address spending at a roundtable meeting for faith-based leaders, she said the county will implement the zero-based budgeting model and focus its attention on what is best for children with regards to spending. Atkinson further noted, however, that she has to first staff on non-negotiable items and train principals to be good leaders in spending funds.

In contrast to the zero-based budgeting model, Cooper says that most school districts use the expenditure model by simply reviewing the revenues and expenditures from the previous year with the understanding that everything is fine. These districts engage in cutting activities from the budget without little or no consideration of what can be cut as oppose to assessing the effectiveness of programs from year to year. They fail to review every budget item at school and determine if the activity was successful or not. Cooper believes that the school budget should be tailored to the needs of students. It should include things that you can measure and evaluate periodically and annually.

Cooper cautions schools from budgeting for one thing and then spending on another. He says that if you budget items for football equipment, then the funds should be spent for football equipment, not pizza. In addition, Cooper cautions schools from cutting funds from the budget when items have already been approved. He says this is a disservice to the school and contradicts the zero-based budgeting process.

Cooper's favorite slogan regarding the zero-based budgeting model is that, "if it is worth doing at all, it is worth doing exceptionally well." He believes that people should view the budgetary process as if they were spending their own money. He believes that school districts should treat the zero-based budgeting model like a business allowing the business plan to drive the process. On the same note, Cooper believes the school improvement plan should drive the process for planning, implementing and measuring school activities for their effectiveness. He emphasizes that if the activities provide favorable outcomes, they demonstrate a return on investment and, consequently, get reinstated for the subsequent year.

So, just as a person working for 30 plus years expects a financial return on investment of those years, the school budgeting process must take into account what is the most favorable return on investment for the dollars being spent. Thus, school leaders must assess the best use of taxpayer's dollars and budget the money as if they are handling their own investments for the future.

Is it time to grade school systems' websites?

When shopping, we sometimes rely on "first impression" to purchase a product. Similarly, parents may rely on this same approach when enrolling their children in various schools. This might include their "first impression" of the grades of students on standardized tests, the grades of parents' involvement in the educational setting and the grades of the school system based on federal standards such as the No Child Left Behind Act.

Since parents can rely on various methods to determine where to enroll their children in school, the questions to be asked are: Is it time to grade school systems' websites? Is there a criterion to grade school systems' websites? What school systems received outstanding grades for their websites?

The Sunshine Review, a national nonprofit organization dedicated to local and state government transparency, grades government agencies such as school systems "that are doing an exemplary job at proactively disclosing information to taxpayers and setting a transparency standard that all governments can and should meet," according to president Michael Barnhart of Sunshine Review.

With the goal of Sunshine Review to make government websites transparent, relevant and accessible to all stakeholders such as parents, editors from Sunshine Review analyzed more than 6,000 government websites and graded them on a 10-point checklist for the 2012 awards. These websites were graded on information pertaining to budgets, meetings, audits, academic performance, public records, etc. Out of the 6,000 websites, the Sunny Awards went to 214 government agencies.

The leading states for the Sunny Awards were Florida, Texas, Illinois, Virginia, Ohio and Pennsylvania. Ten states, including Florida and California, earned an "A" on their school districts' website. In fact, among the 110 school districts' websites evaluated in California, San Francisco United School District (SFUSD) was the only district in this state to earn an "A" grade. SFUSD's multilingual site receives approximately 100,000 unique visitors each month. The district redesigned its website (www.sfusd.edu) through grant funding in 2011 making it more transparent and accessible for students, parents, teachers, administrators, community officials, etc.

In a quick perusal of the website, you can review pertinent information about SFUSD, the public schools affiliated with SFUSD and the enrollment process in the SFUSD schools. In addition, you can learn information about family resources, programs, services, curriculum and standards at SFUSD. This all provides a vehicle to assist parents in making their school choices and gaining the best opportunities for their children.

Florida had the most government agencies to win the Sunny Award and it had the most school districts in the nation to receive an "A" grade on their websites. Some of these school districts included Duval County Public Schools, Escambia County School District, Orange County Public Schools, Palm Beach County School District and St. Johns County School District.

While "first impression" is everything in the perception of people, this can also relate to parents as they rely on various resources to determine where to place their children in school. The Sunshine Review provides a valuable avenue for school districts to compare how their websites are meeting the standards of transparency and accessibility of information to all constituents and particularly parents. School districts' websites provide an important view into what is happening at the school and helps parents form their impressions about the school.

For additional information on all government entities that became recipients of the 2012 Sunny Awards, please visit: http://sunshinereview.org/index. php/2012_Sunny_Awards.

Who should have the power to approve charter schools?

Just as businesses must provide customers a quality product or service, schools must offer students a quality education. When they do not, parents have the right to choose alternatives to educate their children. One alternative is a charter school. This type of school is operated as a school district, part of a school district, for-profit organization or non-profit organization.

To increase public school options, U.S. Secretary of Education Arne Duncan announced in 2010 charter school grant awards totaling $136 million to twelve states. Considering the increasing prevalence of charter schools, the critical questions to be asked are: Who should have the power to approve charter schools? What are the pros and cons of the Georgia charter school amendment?

According to the National Center for Education Evaluation, there are over 5,000 charter schools serving 1.5 million students, representing three percent of all public schools in 40 states and the District of Columbus. Charter schools are the largest vehicle for school choice to parents in America's public schools according to the Center for Research on Education Outcomes.

Charter schools first originated in 1991 through the passing of legislation in Minnesota. These schools are given more autonomy than traditional public schools to create innovative curricula, programs and services to meet the needs of specific students. They are responsible for improving students' achievement according to established goals of their charters or contracts as negotiated between the governing bodies such as local school boards, state education agencies, universities and business organizations. They must meet the goals of the charters in order to continue operating.

States such as Florida and Georgia have advocated for the power to approve charter schools in addition to local authorities. In 2008, the Florida Supreme Court rejected a law that would allow approval of charter schools at the state level. In 2011, Florida lawmakers approved a policy for the implementation of virtual charter schools. In 2012, the Florida State Board of Education overruled the decisions of local school boards in Volusia, Orange, Seminole, Polk and Brevard counties to disapprove virtual charter and other charter school applications. The districts argued that the applications fell short of acceptable standards.

Similarly, the Georgia Supreme Court in 2011 overturned the use of a state commission to approve and oversee charter schools. To overcome legal ramifications, Georgia lawmakers approved a ballot referendum for the November 2012 election that gave voters the opportunity to approve a change in the constitution to decide whether or not a state commission should have the power to create charter schools over the objection of local school boards.

Georgia voters approved the charter school amendment where the new commission will have the authority to address appeals of local charter school applications or review and approve applications directly through its commission. Some voters complained that the language of the amendment ("Shall the Constitution of Georgia be amended to allow state or local approval of public charter schools upon the request of local communities?") was confusing and distorted the real intent of the proposal.

According to charter school proponents, the passing of the amendment places more power in the hands of parents for school choice, gives charter applicants more alternatives for approval and helps to improve accountability for student performance. On the other hand, charter school opponents noted that the approval of the new state commission diverts local control over schools, increases an avenue for private companies to run public schools for a profit and takes money away from underfunded public schools already impacted by yearly budget cuts.

Republican Governor Nathan Deal advocated for the charter school amendment while Georgia PTA and Republican state superintendent, John Barge opposed the amendment. Local school boards in Gainesville City and Hall County Schools publicly opposed the amendment. Dr. Merrianne Dyer, superintendent of Gainesville City Schools said, "We did not want the amendment to pass because of the funding and the creation of another layer of bureaucracy for education, but now that the citizens of Georgia have spoken, we feel confident we can meet the challenge."

While there appears to be a plethora of federal resources such as charter school grants to improve America's schools, we must ensure that the resources are funneled equally to our future workforce (the students) in the rural, urban and suburban communities so students are prepared for college and careers. Having the power to approve charter schools should be the decision of taxpayers. However, voters should be properly informed about the reasons for their voting so they make the best decision about funding education for our children.

Regarding Higher Education

How should general counsel be used at colleges and universities?

At our colleges and universities, there is always the potential for legal issues regarding stakeholders on policies, programs, activities, etc. As we know there are foreseeable problems, the critical questions to be asked are: How should general counsel be used at colleges and universities? What are some of the legal cases in higher education that require the involvement of general counsel? What is the legal issue regarding the Fisher v. Texas case?

While attending the 95th American Council on Education (ACE) Conference in Washington, D.C., a panel of experts discussed legal issues confronting presidents at colleges and universities. The panel members included moderator and general counsel for ACE, Ada Meloy; Jonathan R. Alger, president of James Madison University; Pamela Brooks Gann, president of Claremont McKenna College and Martin Michaelson, partner in the law practice at Hogan Lovells.

One particular topic the panel spoke about was the necessity of general counsel being an integral part of the administrative leadership team in higher education. Alger, for instance, said that he brought a general counsel into his leadership cabinet utilizing the lawyer's ability to "help spot and litigate issues." He expressed that lawyers can be your best friends and recommended that they become actively involved with the National Association of College and University Attorneys (NACUA) for legal assistance. He says that institutions can best use lawyers by posing question, "Here is what we are trying to accomplish, how do we get there?"

Similarly, Brooks Gann said that she developed a general counsel staff position for her institution, placed the person in her leadership cabinet and allowed the lawyer to be involved with risk management issues (healthcare, fringe benefits, etc.), crisis management and sensitive correspondences. Michaelson noted that an "institution's letters should not look like they are written by lawyers, and they should be clear and short" rather than vague and ambiguous. He also recognized that a general counsel position is really needed to address higher education issues because risk management alone is a "daunting task." The compelling opinion of the panel was that higher education should not be any different than corporate America. According to the Association of Corporate Counsel, 75 percent of general counsels report to executive officers in the business sector, said Meloy.

Further, the panel discussed the Fisher v. Texas legal case which requires the involvement, understanding, expertise and guidance of general counsel in higher education. As context, in the Fisher v. Texas case, plaintiffs Abigail Fisher and Rachel Multer Michalewicz (both white females) applied to the University of Texas at Austin (UT) in 2008 but were denied admission. Fisher and Michalewicz filed suit, alleging that UT had discriminated against them on the basis of their race in violation of the Equal Protection Clause of the Fourteenth Amendment. In 2011, Michalewicz withdrew from the case leaving Fisher as the remaining plaintiff. UT admits applicants in the top 10 percent of each high school graduation class in Texas regardless of race. Fisher was in the top 12 percent of her high school class.

On February 21, 2012, the Supreme Court agreed to hear the case. Justice Elena Kagan has recused herself from the case. In support of Fisher and UT, many groups have filed amicus briefs. According to Meloy, 11 groups filed on behalf of Fisher such as the Texas Association of Scholars and the American Civil Rights Union; and 71 filed on behalf of the UT including the NAACP, Legal Defense and Educational Fund and American Council on Education. ACE filed on the basis of the University of Michigan case (Grutter v. Bollinger) and specifically asserted that "the educational benefits that come from a diverse student body are a compelling government interest and institutions must be allowed to make autonomous decisions when determining the composition of their student bodies."

While the outcome remains to be determined, the panel provided the attendees at the session (chancellors, presidents, lawyers, chief academic officers and diversity officers) with some food for thought in terms of what the Supreme Court might consider in making a decision. The panel mentioned or inferred questions such as: How do you define merit? How should your program or admissions policy look? Why is the program or admissions policy relevant since we have an African-American president? How much deference will be given? How do you adhere to a critical mass? How many minority students are enough? Is the percentage admissions plan of the UT system sufficient? What is the educational mission of the institution? What is the possible outcome? (loss of institutional accountability, affirmative action, etc.). With Justice Kagan's recusal, what impact would this have on the case?

Considering the preponderance of legal issues in higher education, presidents should include legal counsel as a part of their leadership cabinet. Presidents should provide training to all stakeholders associated with their campuses for preventive measures as well as improvement of practices. They should use NACUA for legal assistance and resources. They should also use the Higher Education Compliance Alliance for information and resources to comply with federal laws and regulations.

What new mindsets are needed to harness change?

The new mantra in business is that the only thing that stays constant is change. Change is inevitable and is the new norm for our world. Just as businesses have to deal with change, our educational institutions need to embrace and harness the dynamics of change. For education, the questions to be asked are: What new mindsets are needed to harness change and how can we do this considering the economic climate of finite resources.

The theme for the 95th Annual Meeting of the American Council on Education (ACE) was "Leading Change." The keynote speaker for the opening session was Dr. William E. (Brit) Kirwan, chancellor, for the University System of Maryland. Following are excerpts from Kirwan's address on the new mindsets needed by the educational community:

Need for educated parents

Kirwan notes that in our society, a college degree is essential. A person with a college degree earns over one million dollars more than a person with a high school diploma. However, too many disadvantaged children are not going to college. And, they have a 29 percent less chance of enrolling in higher education if their parents do not have a degree. A child born into a family at the highest quartile of income, has an 85 percent chance of earning a degree compared to less than an eight percent chance for a child born into a family at the lowest quartile of income. Based on these statistics, Kirwan believes that education is dependent upon having an educated parent base. Without this base, we have a permanent economic underclass.

Leading change

Throughout American history, we have been confronted with challenges. During these times, we have had incredible leaders such as president Abraham Lincoln and civil rights leader, Reverend Martin Luther King, Jr. to "lead change and take risk to secure the nation's well being" for a better future for all humankind. Our nation needs the higher education community to lead change as never before. We do not have enough students pursuing STEM (Science Technology Engineering and Mathematics) degrees although these skills are essential for a 21st century workforce. According to the National Science Foundation, this crisis of having a skilled labor force threatens American security.

The New Mindset

Kirwan believes that to harness change without spending additional revenues will "require a new mindset." He reveals that we can lead change through four areas: (1) more effective matching of students with colleges; (2) employing different financial aid models; (3) building a stronger culture of college completion rates; and (4) utilizing online teaching to provide lower cost, high quality education.

College Matching:

Kirwan states that an alarming number of students do not attend colleges and, particularly, institutions suited or tailored best for their needs as cited in the book, "Crossing the Finish Line" by William G. Bowen, Matthew M. Chingos and Michael S. McPherson. Kirwan says that students such as African-Americans should attend colleges that better match their needs and the institutions need to do a better job of serving them. Further, Kirwan emphasizes a need to create stronger partnerships with middle and high schools in economically disadvantaged school districts such as the Way to Go Maryland Program. This program encourages middle and high school students to begin preparation for college early and offers tips for parents.

Financial Aid:

Kirwan notes that the U.S. Department of Education is seeking new ideas from the higher education community on the policies and practices for financial aid. According to Kirwan, several organizations have expressed a need to end financial aid awards to students upon the completions of 125 credits, extend disbursement over a longer period of time and award students for substantial progress towards completions.

College Completion:

Kirwan says that we do a good job of "advertising to attract students to colleges;" however, we do not commit the same attention to ensuring that students graduate from our institutions. He recommends that we benchmark best practices with institutions that are having success with graduation rates such as the University of Northern Iowa, Pennsylvania State, Albany State and Florida State Universities. According to a study conducted by Kati Haycock and the Education Trust, these universities have success rates that are approximately 11-20 percentage points higher than their peer institutions. Kirwan says the key to their institutions is that their presidents "made a visible focus and commitment to college completion."

Resources:

As a part of any successful institution, effective leaders learn how to take advantage of available resources. In an information age, Kirwan says we have to maximize the use of technology and if we don't change the way we operate, we do not have a realistic hope of offering high quality education at a lower cost. As an example, Kirwan referenced Carol Twigg, president of the National Center for Academic Transformation. Twigg uses information technology such as online learning to transform teaching and learning in higher education while reducing instructional costs.

As we embark upon this 21st century, the only constant is change. For educators, we must either lead the change or be lead. Kirwan's ending question to the educational community is key, "Do we have the will to lead change?"

What is the Supreme Court ruling of the Fisher v. Texas legal case?

One of America's schools responsibilities is to prepare students for higher education. As a part of that process, students must meet certain admission standards of educational institutions. At the same time, these institutions must establish admission polices that are fair to all students. So, the critical questions to be asked are: What is the Supreme Court ruling of the Fisher v. Texas legal case? What is the legal background of the Abigail Fisher v. University of Texas at Austin (UT)? How does UT admit student applicants to its institution?

In the Fisher v. Texas case, plaintiff Abigail Fisher (white female) applied to the University of Texas at Austin (UT) in 2008 but was denied admission. Fisher filed suit, alleging that UT had discriminated against her on the basis of race in violation of the Equal Protection Clause of the Fourteenth Amendment. UT admits applicants in the top 10 percent of each high school graduation class in Texas regardless of race. Fisher was in the top 12 percent of her high school class. She was one of 29,501 applicants to apply for admissions at UT. From this pool, 12,843 applicants were admitted excluding Fisher.

In support of Fisher and UT, many groups filed amicus briefs prior to the Supreme Court ruling. On behalf of Fisher, some of the groups included the Texas Association of Scholars, the American Center for Law and Justice and the American Civil Rights Union. On behalf of UT, some of the groups included the

Association of American Law Schools, the Society of American Law Teachers and the American Council on Education.

On Monday, June 24, 2013, the Supreme Court ruled in a 7-1 decision on the Fisher v. Texas legal case related to affirmative action in college admissions. The court cited that the policy of admitting the top 10 percent of each high school graduation class in Texas regardless of race needs greater scrutiny than what was provided by the Fifth U.S. Court of Appeals. The Supreme Court ordered a federal appeals court in Texas to reconsider the case and review closely UT's criteria for admitting students. The Supreme Court referenced several cases as framework for the federal appeals court to "assess whether UT has offered sufficient evidence to prove that its admission program is narrowly tailored to obtain the educational benefits of diversity."

In trying to interpret the ramification of the court decision, some opponents of affirmative action postulate that the Supreme Court ruling creates a path for the appeals court to reject UT's admissions policy. On the other hand, proponents of affirmative action express the idea that colleges in some instances can consider race in college admissions. However, they have to show how considering race or diversity in college admissions is essential to their educational mission. From the opinion of a panel of lawyers at the American Council on Education's 95th Annual Meeting, this legal case raises the following challenges for the federal appeals court to measure: How do you define merit? How should college program or admissions policy look? How much deference will be given? How do you adhere to a critical mass? How many minority students are enough? Is the percentage admissions plan of the UT system sufficient? What is the educational mission of the institution?

As we continue to wait for a final ruling of the Fisher v. Texas legal case, educational institutions must establish admission policies that are fair to all students. For legal assistance and resources, they should contact the National Association of College and University Attorneys and the Higher Education Compliance Alliance.

How can the nation's higher education be restored to preeminence?

U.S. students are not completing high school and college at a productive level to fuel our economy. In fact, the gap between what students need to know in high school versus college is widening. This is disturbing when you consider the highest paying jobs require rigorous training or a college education. It is also disturbing when you consider the unemployment figure is 8.9 percent for college graduates with bachelor degrees, 22.9 percent for high school graduates and 31.5 percent for high school dropouts according to a study by the Georgetown Center on Education and Workforce. In reviewing this dilemma, the critical questions to be asked are: How can the nation's higher education be restored to preeminence? What is the blueprint to improve retention and completion for postsecondary educational attainment?

In 2011, the National Commission on Higher Education Attainment was created to chart a course for greatly improving college retention and attainment and, in turn, restore the nation's higher education to preeminence. Through the appointment of six presidential higher education associations, the commission is comprised of 18 members including presidents from community colleges, research institutions, state and independent colleges and universities, as well as public and land grant institutions. As of the Spring Semester 2013, the commission is led by president E. Gordon Gee of The Ohio State University, president Andrew K. Benton of Pepperdine University, president Gail Mellow of LaGuardia Community College, president George Pruitt of Thomas Edison State College and president Molly Corbett Broad of the American Council on Education.

On January 23, 2013, the commission released an open letter to college and university leaders indicating that college completion must be our priority and for the leaders to call upon their colleagues to make retention and completion a critical priority to stem the unacceptable loss of human potential represented by the number of students who never make it to graduation. With the U.S. goal to have the highest proportion of postsecondary educational attainment in the world by 2020, the commission's open letter discussed a blueprint for a campus-level college completion campaign designed to prevent students from failing to obtain a college degree.

For college and university leaders, the commission urged them to consider changing the campus culture, improve cost-effectiveness and quality and make better use of data. The commission open letter also included possible strategies to advance the goal of increased attainment by assigning responsibility to specific senior administrators at our nation's colleges and universities to improve retention and graduation rates, improve remedial services, pinpoint weaknesses in preparation, expand the use of assessments that measure learning acquired outside the traditional classroom and harness information technology to identify at-risk students. Commission Chair E. Gordon Gee said, "While America boasts an unequaled system of higher education, we cannot afford to squander the opportunity it represents to millions of Americans. We must broaden the national conversation about higher education. It is incumbent upon campus leaders to ensure that completion is as much of an institutional priority as access."

Similar to the National Commission on Higher Education Attainment, the Common Core State Standards (CCSS) were adopted in 2009 and 2010 by the National Governors Association Center for Best Practices and the Council of Chief State School Officers for elementary and secondary schools. Forty-eight states, two territories and the District of Columbia are participating in the program. Through the input of teachers, school administrators and other stakeholders across the political spectrum, the CCSS were developed to provide a clear and concise framework to prepare students in the K-12 environment for college and careers.

In a 2012 statement to support the importance of students being prepared for the workforce, Robert Corcoran, Vice President of GE Corporate Citizenship and

President and Chair of GE Foundation said, "our economy is facing an undeniable challenge—good paying jobs are going unfilled because U.S. workers don't have the skills to fill the positions." To illustrate the point, Corcoran noted that its GE Transportation plant in Erie, Pennsylvania posted 25 jobs in manufacturing and engineering, received thousands of applications for people seeking the manufacturing jobs such as making parts but only a hand full of people applied for the engineering jobs. Thus, Corcoran concluded, "We must cultivate a highly educated workforce, and we see the Common Core State Standards as a key component to answering this challenge."

The economy is in demand of a competent and competitive workforce and American schools, colleges and universities must rise to the standards. The National Commission on Higher Education Attainment has created a course to greatly improve the college retention and attainment to restore the nation's higher education to preeminence. Just like any monumental challenge, there can be no one-size-fits-all method of operation. Whatever methods are chosen, it will require the schools, colleges and universities to work hand in hand to create workable solutions for educating our students for a challenging workforce environment.

How do we increase the diversity of business school faculty?

With a disproportionate number of minorities in corporate jobs, diversity and inclusion are essential to the vitality of the workforce. At the corporate boardrooms level, nearly 4.2 percent of the executives are people of color. Specifically, the numbers are 0.8 percent for African-Americans, 1.2 percent for Latinos and 1.8 percent for Asians according to the Center for American Progress.

Considering this staggering disparity in corporate jobs, the critical questions to be asked are: What is The PhD Project? What are the benefits for a doctoral student being recruited by The PhD Project? How does increasing the diversity of business school faculty impact the diversity of professions in corporate jobs? To address these questions, I interviewed Bernard J. Milano, president of The PhD Project who played a significant role in leading an effort to increase the academic and professional development of minorities in mid-careers.

Founded in 1994 by the KPMG Foundation, The PhD Project is a 501 (c) (3) organization that recruits minority professionals from business into doctoral programs in such disciplines as finance, accounting, management, marketing and information systems. Historically, very few minority college students study business as an entrée to a corporate career. The Project attacks the root cause of minority under-representation in corporate jobs according to Milano. He says that "if you don't have a minority faculty in the educational setting, you are not going to attract minority students. If you do have minority students, it is not going to be a comfortable environment for minority students if the faculty and student body are majority students. So we are trying to change the educational environment suitable to the environment students will be expected to live and work in."

The Project currently has 361 minorities enrolled in doctoral programs at various universities. Since its inception, the number of minority business professors (African-American, Hispanic-American and Native American) has quadrupled from 294 to 1,217. Milano says this is due largely to the efforts of The Project. Ninety-seven percent of the professors are members on the faculty at business schools throughout the U.S. He believes that by diversifying the faculty, this attracts more minorities to study business and better prepares all students to function in a diverse workforce.

With the support of over 20 co-funders from top U.S. companies, foundations, associations and academic organizations (Microsoft Corporation, JP Morgan Chase Foundation, American Accounting Association, Graduate Management Admission Council, etc.), The Project encourages highly qualified professionals who are considering leaving their careers to enter doctoral business programs. Milano says that The Project's website provides a wealth of information about the program to address candidates' initial interests, questions and concerns before making a decision.

Candidates with a sincere interest are invited to The Project's fall conference where over 100 universities are present allowing them to hear from professors, deans and current minority doctoral students about the process of pursuing a Ph.D. in business. Candidates also learn about career opportunities in higher education as a business doctoral graduate.

For admission consideration, doctoral programs at various universities look at past academic achievement and rely heavily on the scores achieved on the GMAT, as well as letters of recommendations that reflect on the candidates' approach to problem solving and intellectual curiosity. According to Milano, a master's degree or MBA is not required to enter the doctoral program. Candidates in the program currently represent people from business, public sector, law, engineering, as well as people directly from undergraduate schools.

Once accepted into a full-time doctoral program, every minority business doctoral student in an AACSB accredited U.S. business school becomes a member of one of The Project's five Doctor Student Associations (DSA): finance, accounting, management, marketing and information systems. Each year, The Project holds separate annual conferences for each of the DSA disciplines, providing the candidates with a strong support network and tools to help them navigate through their doctoral programs. The conferences are typically held in the summer before new candidates start the programs, but candidates at all levels in their programs attend each year. All conference expenses are covered by The Project, says Milano.

For additional information about The PhD Project, visit the website: www. phdproject.org/.

Roadmap for Successful & Struggling Schools in the U.S.

Introduction

America's schools are faced with numerous challenges in today's society such as the lack of family stability and involvement; the alarming number of food insecure households; the high truancy, suspension, expulsion rates and criminal offenses of juvenile delinquents; the peer pressure; the safety and security of schools; the offering of a well-balanced curriculum for all students; the selection of effective school leaders and teachers; the grading of schools and the budgetary shortfalls.

Problem Statement

The challenges of America's schools are leading to a significant number of students not graduating from school. Annually, about 1.2 million students drop out of school which equates to 7,000 students dropping out each school day or one child every 26 seconds. Some of the reasons for the drop out rate include students' failure to pass high school exit exams, home environment, poverty, peer pressure, poor academic achievement, low teacher and parental involvement, school curriculum and discipline, violence, drugs and criminal offenses.

Solution to Problem

The problems of America's schools are contributing to the failure of struggling schools throughout the United States. After analyzing thoroughly in 2011 four struggling or intervene schools in Duval County Public Schools (DCPS), I, on behalf of the National Save the Family Now Movement, Inc., proposed various components of the following information on the next page to DCPS as a solution to address the academic and social concerns in the intervene schools. I also designed this roadmap to provide the vision for successful and struggling schools throughout the U.S.

ROADMAP FOR SUCCESSFUL & STRUGGLING SCHOOLS IN THE U.S.

2014

ACTION PLAN

Ronald W. Holmes, Ph.D.

National Superintendent of Education

National Save the Family Now Movement, Inc.

Vision

To meet Adequate Yearly Progress (AYP), state assessment exams, and other state standards for successful & struggling schools in the U.S. The following is the roadmap for achieving this vision.

ROADMAP FOR SUCCESSFUL & STRUGGLING SCHOOLS IN THE U.S.

Objective 1: Implementation of Curriculum & Technology in the Classroom

GOAL:

Provide rigorous curriculum with emphasis on English/Language Arts, science, technology, and math in accordance with state-wide testing standards, Common Core State Standards and instructional learning resources

STRATEGIES:

Recruit teachers capable of teaching rigorous curriculum; provide training on state testing standards, Common Core State Standards and specific instructional models such as Whole Brain Instruction and Learning Focused Strategies; offer Cambridge Advanced International Certification Education (AICE); provide Computer-Aided Instruction; utilize Online Learning to expand the curriculum; and install technology in the classroom (wireless network, Smart Boards, parent connect, i.e.) to produce technology capable students

PERFORMANCE MEASURES:

AICE, test scores, and Computer-Aided Instruction such as Khan Academy, Pearson Success Maker, Waterford Learning System, Laptop usage, Wireless writing pads, and iPods

BOOK REFERENCES:

Your Answers to Education Questions: Article, "What makes DISD's School for the Talented and Gifted the Top in the Nation?"

Education Questions to be Answered: Article, "Do cellular telephones enhance or impede the learning process at school?"

Current Issues and Answers in Education: Article, "What makes Thomas Jefferson High School of Science and Technology successful?"

ROADMAP FOR SUCCESSFUL & STRUGGLING SCHOOLS IN THE U.S.

Objective 2: Improvement of Student Achievement on Standardized Tests

GOALS:

Align expectations of student achievement in English/Language Arts, math, science and social studies to the Common Core State Standards

Prepare student for state tests in subject areas such as English/Language Arts, math, science and social studies at or above grade level expectations

STRATEGIES:

Provide training to teachers on all instructional standards and models to improve teaching and learning such as Common Core State Standards and Learning-Focused Strategies; use Computer Aided Instruction; Offer After School and Saturday Enrichment Academies for core areas; and provide incentives to students for exemplary performance in conduct, academics and on standardized exams.

PERFORMANCE MEASURES:

Student Performance on State Tests, Classroom Assessments, Observations and Computer Aided Systems

BOOK REFERENCES:

Your Answers to Education Questions: Article, "Is it time for more after school and summer learning programs?"

Education Questions to be Answered: Article, "How can schools better assess students' learning?"

Current Issues and Answers in Education: Article, "How did two Atlanta area schools consistently make AYP and become Georgia's 2011 Title I Distinguished Schools?"

ROADMAP FOR SUCCESSFUL & STRUGGLING SCHOOLS IN THE U.S.

Objective 3: Coordination of Professional Development

GOAL:

Implementation of training on the Common Core State Standards

STRATEGIES:

Train Faculty on Common Core State Standards and instructional models such as Learning-Focused Strategies during the Summer and Pre-Planning, as well as training on professional learning communities, Whole Brain Instruction, the integration of technology in the curriculum, and state reading and math diagnostic tools. Also, provide training to school administrator on standards from the Interstate School Leaders Licensure Consortium; and implement a rigorous evaluation plan in line with the curriculum focus.

PERFORMANCE MEASURES:

Classroom Assessment, Teacher/Faculty Observation, and Student Performance

BOOK REFERENCES:

Your Answers to Education Questions: Article, "How can schools use employees' strengths to improve performance in the workforce?"

Education Questions to be Answered: Article, "What are the leadership standards for school leaders and how should they be measured?"

Current Issues and Answers in Education: Article, "Is there a fair evaluation system for grading teachers?"

ROADMAP FOR SUCCESSFUL & STRUGGLING SCHOOLS IN THE U.S.

Objective 4: Recruitment & Retention of Students

GOAL:

Provide a strong commitment to Student Focus & Support

STRATEGIES:

Offer rigorous curriculum in Honors, DE, IB, AICE, SAT, ACT & IC; establish community service activities; provide co-& extra-curricular activities; establish student exchange program, career day & college tours; implement a researched-based reading program; provide incentives for exemplary student attendance and conduct; implement after school and Saturdays enrichment academies; and provide students access to The Holmes Education Post

PERFORMANCE MEASURES:

Course Offerings, Innovative Programs, Student Awards & Recognition for excellent attendance, conduct, academic achievement, and community service activities

BOOK REFERENCES:

Your Answers to Education Questions: Articles, "What should be the civic mission of U.S. public schools?" "Why are some students less likely to take AP courses?"

Education Questions to be Answered: Articles, "Do AP, IB, or AICE courses determine America's Best High Schools?" "How can extra-curriculum activities contribute to student achievement?"

Current Issues and Answers in Education: Article, "Can hip-hop music in the curriculum influence African-American students to learn?"

ROADMAP FOR SUCCESSFUL & STRUGGLING SCHOOLS IN THE U.S.

Objective 5: Recruitment of Highly Qualified Faculty

GOAL:

Foster a strong commitment to Faculty Growth and Development

STRATEGIES:

Provide competitive salaries and Merit Pay Program; provide incentives for pursuing National Board Certification; offer continuous professional development opportunities; provide teachers access to The Holmes Education Post; incorporate mentoring program including the utilization of retired teachers; and build partnership or team building relations

PERFORMANCE MEASURES:

Innovative Programs, Faculty Awards and Recognition for excellent attendance, teaching, and community service activities

BOOK REFERENCES:

Your Answers to Education Questions: Article, "What is an alternative to teacher certification?

Education Questions to be Answered: Article, "Is it time to pay teachers more money? If so, how should it be done?"

Current Issues and Answers in Education: Article, "What is the purpose of the Common Core State Standards?"

ROADMAP FOR SUCCESSFUL & STRUGGLING SCHOOLS IN THE U.S.

Objective 6: Implementation of Parental Involvement Model

GOAL:

Enlist parents to become an integral part of the school

STRATEGIES:

Establish a parent involvement (pledge) contract; provide parents access to Online Parent Connect System to students' grades, homework, attendance; provide parents access to The Holmes Education Post; provide professional development activities for parents; host parent meetings in the community; offer online learning opportunities; and implement community service activities

PERFORMANCE MEASURES:

Surveys, school meetings, events, and workshops

BOOK REFERENCES:

Your Answers to Education Questions: Article, "How can school districts create a culture of excellence for all students, staff and families?"

Education Questions to be Answered: Articles, "How can Parent University increase parental involvement?" "How do we get parents back in the schools?"

Current Issues and Answers in Education: Article, "Is it time to grade parents in school?"

ROADMAP FOR SUCCESSFUL & STRUGGLING SCHOOLS IN THE U.S.

Objective 7: Creation of Business/Community Partnerships

GOAL:

Establishment of partnerships linked to student achievement

STRATEGIES:

Establish partnerships with State Educational Agency, College Board, universities and colleges, local agencies, companies, corporations, foundations, churches, retired teachers, Greek organizations, and feeder schools

PERFORMANCE MEASURES:

Partnership Agreement Form, meetings, activities, and recognition events

BOOK REFERENCES:

Your Answers to Education Questions: Articles, "Is it time to bailout U.S. school districts? "How can schools improve educational opportunities for military students?"

Education Questions to be Answered: Article, "How does vertical alignment improve student performance in the schools?"

Current Issues and Answers in Education: Article, "How do thousands of baby fish graduate from school?"

ROADMAP FOR SUCCESSFUL & STRUGGLING SCHOOLS IN THE U.S.

Objective 8: Establishment of Organizational Climate

GOAL:

Creation of a safe and collaborative atmosphere conducive for improved teaching & learning

STRATEGIES:

Implement best practices of the Blue Ribbon School of Excellence, Inc. Model; establish a dress code for students and faculty; implement Arthur Costa's 16 habits of the mind to help students become successful in school; offer an academically challenging learning environment; provide programs and services to meet students' academic, social and physical needs; award incentives for exemplary performance and attendance for both students and faculty; offer flex bell schedules for special programs; establish vertical alignment with feeder schools; incorporate the belief that failure is not an option; and maintain a safe and enriching learning environment

PERFORMANCE MEASURES:

Surveys, Classroom Observations, and Interviews of Stakeholders

BOOK REFERENCES:

Your Answers to Education Questions: Articles, "Is it time to teach kids about stranger safety?" Is it time to stand for the silent?" "Is it time to place cameras in the classroom?"

Education Questions to be Answered: Article, "Should there be a framework for high performing schools?"

Current Issues and Answers in Education: Article, "How can music empower students and a community?"

ROADMAP FOR SUCCESSFUL & STRUGGLING SCHOOLS IN THE U.S.

Objective 9: Employment of Key Personnel to meet state and national requirements

GOAL:

Strive to become a Blue Ribbon School of Excellence

STRATEGIES:

Employ highly qualified educational leaders and teachers to foster a positive learning environment; and employ consultants for training of students, parents, faculty and staff in various areas to improve student achievement

PERFORMANCE MEASURES:

Assessment of school environment, State Educational Agency, and U.S. Department of Education

BOOK REFERENCES:

Your Answers to Education Questions: Article, "How did Douglas County School District avoid a budget cut?"

Education Questions to be Answered: Article, "What are the leadership standards for school leaders and how should they be measured?"

Current Issues and Answers in Education: Article, Is it time to privatize public education?

ROADMAP FOR SUCCESSFUL & STRUGGLING SCHOOLS IN THE U.S.

Objective 10: Evaluation of School's Organization

GOAL:

Maintain management accountability

STRATEGIES:

Formulate written agreement with State Educational Agency; promote open lines of communication with State Educational Agency; and demonstrate periodically evidence of activities in agreement being fulfilled

PERFORMANCE MEASURES:

Records of reports, newsletter, meetings notes, board hearings, portfolios, programs and services

BOOK REFERENCES:

Your Answers to Education Questions: Article, "How can school districts benefit from a zero-based budgeting model?"

Education Questions to be Answered: Article, "What are the standards of the Accreditation Agency for school systems?"

Current Issues and Answers in Education: Article, "Is it time to fix the No Child Left Behind Act?"

REFERENCES

After School Alliance (2013). *The importance of afterschool and summer learning programs in African-American and Latino Communities. Retrieved October 28, 2013 from,* http://www.afterschoolalliance.org/ issue_59_African-American_and_Latino_Communities.cfm

Alfred University (2012). *Hazing policy. Retrieved October 28, 2013 from,* http:// my.alfred.edu/ index.cfm/fuseaction/student_policies.hazing_0708.cfm

Allan, E. J. & Madden, M. (2008). *Hazing in view: College students at risk. Initial findings from the national study of student hazing. Retrieved October 28, 2013 from,* http://www.epi. soe.vt.edu/ perspectives/policy_news/ pdf/hazingstudy.pdf

Alliance for Excellent Education (2011). *Fact sheet: high school dropout in America. Retrieved October 28, 2013 from, Alliance for Excellent Education:* http:// www.aa14ed.org

American Commonweatlth Partnership. *National initiative promoting higher education's civic mission. Retrieved October 28, 2013 from,* http:// democracyu.wordpress.com/about/

American Council on Education (2013). *President to president special edition: ACE filing amicus brief in Fisher v. University of Texas at Austin. Retrieved October 28, 2013, from,* http://www.acenet. edu/president-to-president/ Pages/SPECIAL-Brief-Fisher-UT-Austin. aspx

America's Promise Alliance (2009). *Grad nation: a guidebook to help communities tackle the dropout crisis. Retrieved October 28, 2013 from,* http:// www.americaspromise.org/~/media/Files/ Our%20Work/Dropout%20 Prevention/Grad%20Nation%20Guidebook%20052809.ashx

Association of American Colleges and Universities (2009). *Civic learning and democratic engagement. Retrieved October 28, 2013 from,* http:// ww.aacu.org/civic_learning/ index.cfm

Ballotpedia. 2012 Sunny Awards. Retrieved October 28, 2013 from, http:// ballotpedia.org/wiki/ index. php/2012_Sunny _Awards

Bullying statistics. (2011). Retrieved March 30, 2011, from Behavioral Management: http://behavioral- mannagement.com/bullying-statistics

Campaign for the Civic Mission of Schools. Educating for democracy. Retrieved October 28, 2013 from, http://www.civicmissionofschools.org/

Center for American Progress (2013). The state of diversity in today's workforce. Retrieved October 28, 2013 from, http://www.americanprogress. org/issues/labor/report/2012/ 07/12/11938/the-state-of-diversity-in-todays-workforce/

Center of Budget and Policy Priorities (2012). States continue to feel recession's impact. Retrieved October 28, 2013 from, http://www.cbpp.org/files/2-8-08sfp.pdf

Chudowsky. N. & Gayler, R. (2003). Effects of high school exit exams on dropout rates: summary of a panel discussion. Washington, DC: Center for Education Policy.

Content Marketing Institute (2013). What is content marketing? Retrieved October 28, 2013 from, http://contentmarketinginstitute.com/what-is-content-marketing/

College Board (2011). AP STEM access program Retrieved October 28, 2013 from, http://www. collegeboard.org/ap-stem-access-program.html?excmpid= SM48-ED-CB-tw

College Board (2013). AP students. Retrieved October 28, 2013 from, https:// apstudent.collegeboard.org/home

Department of Defense Educational Activity. Military K-12 partners. Retrieved October 28, 2013 from, http://www.militaryk12partners.dodea.edu/ grants.cfm

Finlayson, K. J. (2009). Perceptions of career technical education by middle school and high school counselors and the effect of these perceptions on student choice of career and education planning. Retrieved October 28, 2013 from http://eric.ed.gov/? id=ED513967

Fox News (2013). Missouri high school reportedly to use hair sampling for random drug tests. Retrieved October 28, 2013 from, http://www.foxnews.com/us/2013/01/31/missouri-high-school-reportedly-to-use-hair-samples-for-random-drug-tests/

Georgetown Center on Education and Workforce (2012). New report finds that risk of unemployment varies by college major. Retrieved October 28, 2013 from, http://www.prnewswire.com/news-releases/new-report-finds-that-risk-of-unemployment-varies-by-college-major-136651868.html

Georgetown Center on Education and Workforce (2012). Hard times, college majors, Unemployment and earnings: not all college degrees are created equal. Retrieved October 28, 2013 from, http://cew.georgetown.edu/unemployment/

Georgia Department of Education (2013). College and Career Readiness Index. Retrieved October 28, 2013 from, http://www.gadoe.org/CCRPI/Pages/default.aspx

Global Post (2013). Facts and statistics on random drug testing of high school students. Retrieved October 28, 2013 from, http://everydaylife.globalpost.com/statistics-random-drug-testing-high-school-students-8400.html

Hirsch, L. (2012). The Bully Project. Retrieved October 28, 2013 from, http://www.thebullyproject.com/

Holmes, R. (2011). Education questions to be answered. Bloomington: AuthorHouse.

Holmes, R. (2012). Current issues and answers in education. Bloomington: AuthorHouse.

iSAFE (2012). Cyber Bullying: Statistics and Tips. Retrieved October 28, 2013 from, http://www.isafe. org/ outreach/media/media_cyber_bullying

Military Child Education Coalition (2012). Retrieved October 28, 2013 from, http://www.militarychild.org

National Association of State Directors of Career Technical Education Consortium. The 16 Career Clusters. Retrieved October 28, 2013 from, http://www.careertech.org/career-clusters/glance/ careerclusters.html

National Center for Education Evaluation (2010). The effectiveness of mandatory-random student drug testing. Retrieved October 28, 2013 from, http://ies.ed.gov/ncee/pubs/ 20104025/

National Center for Education Evaluation (2010). The evaluation of charter schools impact. Retrieved October 28, 2013 from, http://ies.ed.gov/ncee/pubs/20104029/pdf/20104029.pdf

National Center for Missing and Exploited Children (2013). Retrieved October 28, 2013 From, http://www.missingkids.com/hom

National Center for Education Statistics. Projections of education statistics to 2018. Retrieved October 28, 2013 from, http://nces.ed.gov/programs/ projections/projections2018/sec5d.asp

National Institute on Drug Use. (2012). Frequently asked questions about drug testing in schools. Retrieved October 28, 2013 from, http://www.drugabuse.gov/related-topics/ drug-testing/faq-drug-testing-in-schools

NBC(2012). My Kid Would Never Do That: Stranger Danger. Retrieved October 28, 2013 from, http://insidedateline.nbcnews.com/_news/2012/08/31/13593192-sep-2-my-kid-would-never-do-that-stranger-danger

New Jersey Department of Education (2013). Christie administration announces positive reporting of New Jersey's first year teacher evaluation pilot program. Retrieved October 18, 2013 from, http://www.state.nj.us/education/news/2013/0205eval.htm

Oakland Tribune (2012). Lakeview Elementary sit-in: Oakland schools police order crowd to disperse. Retrieved October 28, 2013 from, http://

www.insidebayarea.com/oakland/ci_20883030/ lakeview-elementary-sit-oakland-schools-police-order-crowd

Pearson Foundation (2011). Pathways to Prosperity. Retrieved May 23, 2013, from http://www.gse. harvard.edu/news_events/features/2011/ Pathways_to_Prosperity_ Feb2011.pdf

Philadelphia Inquirer (2012). Judge: Pa. must give Chester Upland schools $3.2M. Retrieved October 28, 2013 from, http://articles.philly.com/2012-01-17/ news/30635441_1_ district-students-charter-schools-district-figures

President Obama & the First Lady at the White House conference on bullying prevention (2011). Retrieved March 30, 2011, from The White House: http://www.whitehouse.gov/ search/ site/Bullying

Price, A. G. (2013). Slashing sports: A national study examining the correlation between athletic involvement and academic success. National Interscholastic Athletic Administrators Association

Student Drug-Testing Coalition. How many U.S. schools randomly drug test students? Retrieved October 28, 2013 from, http://www.studentdrugtesting.org/

The McCormick Tribune Foundation (2007). Civic Disengagement in our democracy. Retrieved October 28, 2013 from, htpp://documents. Mccormickfoundation.org/publications/ civicdisengagement.pdf

The National Assessment of Educational Progress (2011). The nation's report card: Civic 2010. Retrieved October 28, 2013 from, http://cq.ngb.org/ content/nagb/assets/documents/ newsroom/ naep-releases/2010-civics/statement-buckley.pdf

The New York Times (2011). Overriding a key education law. Retrieved October 28, 2013 from, http://www.nytimes.com/2011/03/10/ education/10education.html?pagewanted

The New York Times (2013). Differing views on the value of high school tests. Retrieved October 28, 2013 from, http://www.nytimes.com/2013/01/06/ sports/drug-tests-for-high-school-athletes-fuel-debate.html?_r=3&

U.S. Department of Education (2013). Green Ribbon Schools. Retrieved October 28, 2013 from, http://www2.ed.gov/ programs/green-ribbon-schools/index.html

U.S. Department of Education (2012). U.S. Department Of Education calls for action to develop 21st century citizens, strengthen democracy. Retrieved October 28, 2013 from, http://www.ed.gov/news/press-releases/us-department-education-calls-action-develop-21st-century-citizens-strengthen-de

U.S. News and World Report (2013). Best high schools. Retrieved October 28, 2013 from, http://www.usnews.com/education/best-high-schools

Wikipedia (2013). Zero-based budgeting. Retrieved October 28, 2013 from, http://en.wikipedia.org/ wiki/Zero-based_budgeting

AUTHOR'S BACKGROUND

Ronald Holmes is the author of four books: "Education Questions to be Answered," "Current Issues and Answers in Education," "How to Eradicate Hazing" and "Professional Career Paths." He is the sponsoring editor for the landmark book, "Surviving and Thriving: Candid, Real Life Stories of Prostate Cancer."

Ronald Holmes is president and publisher of The Holmes Education Post, an education focused Internet newspaper. His philanthropist spirit and unselfish giving has enabled him to provide free educational resources and publications to educators across the nation. He publishes weekly articles on educational issues and offers unique, researched based solutions, perspectives, best practices and resources to improve public education.

Ronald Holmes is a member of the National Association of School Superintendents, national superintendent of the National Save the Family Now Movement, Inc. and vice president and education editor of Live Communications, Inc. (Capital Outlook Newspaper and WTAL 1450 AM). He earned a Ph.D. in Educational Leadership, a ME.D. in Educational Administration and Supervision and a B.S. in Business Education from Florida A&M University. He also earned a ME.D. in Business Education from Bowling Green State University. He has proven success working from the elementary to the collegiate level.

Ronald Holmes is a native of Jacksonville, Florida and married to Constance Holmes. He is an avid jogger and enjoys competitive races.